Critiques

CRITIQUES

BY

AUGUSTUS RALLI

Author of *Guide to Carlyle*

78487

PR99
.R16C

ESSAY INDEX

BOOKS FOR LIBRARIES PRESS, INC.

FREEPORT, NEW YORK

First published 1927
Reprinted 1966

ACKNOWLEDGMENTS

THE essays in this volume are reprinted from the periodicals in which they first appeared, by the courtesy of the Editors and Proprietors, viz., *Borrow* and *Charlotte Brontë* from the *Fortnightly Review* ; *Emily Brontë*, *The Earthly Paradise*, *The Wessex Novels*, *Swinburne* and *Pater* from the *North American Review* ; *Boswell* from the *Westminster Review*, and portions of *Jane Austen* and *Edward FitzGerald* from *Everyman*.

CONTENTS

Emily Brontë : The Problem of Personality

EMILY BRONTË : THE PROBLEM OF PERSONALITY

EMILY BRONTË is among the great ones whom it is said that we do not know, and the curiosity that seeks to know more of a writer than his works reveal has been condemned as unworthy. We are told that since he has expressed his mind, and so given his best to the world, we should not hunt after mere personal details. That this objection sounds more plausible than it is, and the modern instinct to make biography intimate is not a mistaken one, is the task here set before us to prove.

Let us realize in the beginning that art is a social virtue, that the ultimate reward of all success is social success, and that man is incomplete till he has expressed not only his mind but his personality. The supreme fact of life is personality, and its expression can be attained only by contact with men and women. To win battles, sway senates, discover new lands, write immortal verse : beyond all these, beyond even the mind's satisfaction in exercising its powers, is the approval of such as have done like things, is admission sought and won into the Paradise of this world—the kind glances of fair women and brave men. Disraeli's social success pleased him as much as his political, and there have been great men without personal magnetism, such as the American General Grant, or Jenner of vaccination fame. An aristocracy of pure intellect will never possess the earth, and the unkempt man of genius no longer excites admiring wonder. While man inhabits the earth he consists of body as well as mind ; the ascetic ideal that despises the body as a clog to the spirit is rejected ; and the modern culture of the body implies that it is a means of expressing the soul. Did not Leonardo da Vinci say that one of the two most wonderful sights in the world was the smiling of women ? "[1]

Plato commended the spoken above the written word, because its meaning is strengthened by change of voice, glance of eye, movement of hand ; and we need only revolve in our thoughts a few homely instances to be assured how vain it is to dispart mind and body. A letter cannot compensate for an absent friend, and a bore is a person whose utterances may be foretold. A twice-told tale will weary, and words that passed almost unnoticed may return and rankle in solitude, and again dissolve like a dream when the speaker is beheld once more in the flesh. A child prefers a story told rather than read from a book, and the very word " lecture " is evilly associated. Gloom envelops a company when a person adopts the lecturer's tone, speaking in a manner once removed from the personalities of his hearers, solving the problem by the help of ready made wisdom instead of that generated by the immediate contact of minds. A great orator creates the illusion in each member of his audience that he is spoken to directly ; and a letter writer of genius never loses contact with his correspondent, whether his theme be objective or subjective ; whether it be Cowper analysing his religious melancholy, or Horace Walpole describing the Gordon riots. The Bacon-Shakespeare dispute is not hushed by the argument that we have the plays so it matters little who wrote them ; and the saying once current that not Homer but someone of the same name composed the Homeric poems, is less absurd than it appears.

[1] Quoted by Pater.

THE PROBLEM OF PERSONALITY

The conclusion is that mind and body express each other, and we do not know our fellow-creatures by one alone. Because of the few surviving details of his life we do not know Shakespeare, though through the mouths of his characters we have his thoughts on every subject in the world and beyond. Much of the cloud of darkness surrounding Chatham has been dispelled by the discovery of his latest biographer, Mr. Basil Williams, that he was exceptionally grateful for acts of personal kindness. Modern critics like Mr. T. S. Eliot and Mr. J. Middleton Murry affirm that every mental process has its equivalent in the world of sense ; indeed Mr. Eliot says that *Hamlet* remains obscure because Shakespeare failed to find something in the outer world corresponding to the hero's disgust at his mother's conduct. It pleases us to think that the essence of the immortal biography is contained in Dr. Johnson's stentorian call to his servant Frank for a clean shirt, when Boswell had pleaded successfully with Mrs. Williams and the road to the Wilkes' dinner party lay open.

The lack of objective correlatives places Emily Brontë among the unknown. Yet the task must not be abandoned, even if we make only the slight advance of realizing more fully the difficulties that beset us. If personality is the force proceeding from united soul and body made objective by the difficulties which stay it or which it overcomes, we can learn something by inquiring into the nature of the difficulties. We think of Cowper succumbing in his struggle with the wish to believe ; FitzGerald self-banished from a world he found too hard ; Swift finally baffled in his desire for power and place and retiring to die like a poisoned rat in a hole—to use his own phrase ; Charlotte Brontë vainly seeking love as a refuge from hypochondria : and in consequence we know much of all these. Then we turn to Gibbon or Wordsworth, both of whom realized their personalities objectively—the one in his history, the other in contemplating nature and giving to his thoughts enduring form. Again, we have a middle class such as Byron and Carlyle, who achieved great fame but remained miserable—the one because of his lost social reputation, the other through imperfect faith, and despair at the condition of the world.

With Emily Brontë there is a break between the operations of her mind as her books reveal it and the few biographical facts that have come down to us. We know that she was the least accessible of the three sisters of genius in the remote Haworth parsonage. She refused all acquaintance beyond her family, and yet was passionately interested in the fortunes of the people about her. As Charlotte says : " She knew their ways, their language, their family histories ; she could hear of them with interest, and talk of them with detail, minute, graphic, and accurate ; but *with* them she rarely exchanged a word." At school in Brussels she spoke to no one, and although, with Charlotte, she spent her weekly holiday at the house of an English family, she remained throughout impenetrable to friendly advances. Heger remarked upon her capacity for argument, unusual in a man and rare indeed in a woman ; adding that hers was a stubborn tenacity of will which rendered her obtuse to all reasoning where her own wishes or her own sense of right were concerned. Mrs. Gaskell described her as reserved in the least favourable sense of the word ; that is, indifferent if she pleased or not. When she went as pupil to Roe Head and teacher to a school near Halifax, she succumbed to home-sickness, and her year's absence in Brussels was nearly cut short for the same reason. She loved liberty, she enjoyed passionately the lonely moors, and she loved wild animals because they were wild. Even in the small home circle she had a preference, and we doubt if she responded fully to the affection Charlotte lavished upon her. Charlotte described her as intractable, and observed that to advocate one side of a cause would ensure her adoption of the opposite. She began to write poetry without confiding in Charlotte, and was not pleased by Charlotte's chance discovery of her manuscripts. Perhaps her sister Anne, with a lesser mind, had a more receptive nature, and made a better companion to a woman of genius. To the end of Emily's short life the two played the game of make-believe which they called the *Gondal Chronicles*. No summary of facts should omit such harrowing details of her death scene as the silence she opposed to questions as to her state, and her refusal until too late to allow a " poisoning doctor " to come near her.

With every wish to estimate Emily favourably, it is hard to do so with the foregoing facts in mind. Exclusive family affection is not a commending trait, and one who persistently declines friendly advances is apt to forfeit human sympathy. In her last illness, had she no thought for the moral sufferings of her sisters when she refused to answer questions or see a doctor ? And yet it is only fair to recall Charlotte's saying that she was full of ruth for others though without pity on herself. If we turn from Charlotte's direct sayings to her fictitious and therefore suggestive ones, we are equally baffled. Shirley Keeldar was supposed to represent Emily in happier circumstances, and yet, while external things such as the rich dresses she wore are much dwelt upon, we are not helped in the ultimate object of our search— a human soul made more beautiful on earth by the body.

There is enough to stimulate but not satisfy the imagination. We can picture the pleased expression on her face in solitude when anticipating her sisters' home-coming, the smile with which she greeted them, the especial look she reserved for Anne when they found themselves alone. On the reverse side we can picture the despair in her eyes when one after another came the harsh reviews of *Wuthering Heights*. But still we lack the actual collision of soul and sense with the outer world to make the vision real.

EMILY BRONTË:

Life is greater than art, the artist's mind surpasses his work, and the crowd of men, indifferent to art, never desist to seek God in their fellow-creatures, though they may know it not. The example of Emily Brontë suggests two problems especially prominent at the present day : personality and hero-worship. Carlyle taught us that hero-worship is the adamant below which unbelief cannot fall ; and that if you convince a man he is in the presence of a higher soul his knees are automatically loosened in reverence. Lately Marcel Proust remarked that some people think of society as an Indian caste in which you take your place as you are born, but in reality all is due to personality : the humblest can become the friend of princes, and there are many princes whose acquaintance no one desires.

Carlyle preached the doctrine of work ; he predicted a commonwealth of workers, and advised the man who had no work to hide himself ; yet he privately admitted true good breeding to be one of the finest things in the world, and remarked the care of well-bred persons to avoid all unpleasant topics in conversation. The two are contradictory, for the effect of strenuous work—other than artistic—is to materialize, and good breeding can only thrive in the soil of leisure. The kind of character developed by the Victorian professional and business man is an answer to those who plead the dignity of work ; and the modern desire for education in late life is an attempt to restore the balance of the mind which every profession inevitably disturbs. The duty of work is to overcome difficulties ; the powers which it develops are the combative or competitive ; whereas the right use of leisure is to promote the growth of the soul—and the greatest soul is that which has the greatest power to love. Good breeding implies that the material struggle has been concluded generations back, that there is no need to compete with others for means of living and so acquire the habit of preferring things to persons. That a leisured class by attaining a certain mental outlook becomes the symbol of a more perfect life, alone justifies its existence in our distracted modern world, and makes the sight of luxury side by side with poverty at all bearable ; and the toiling millions still feel an instinctive respect for those who dress finely and bear themselves graciously and do no work, despite the Communist orator.

That leisure and accumulated wealth are daily put to the worst uses is a truth we will not stay to consider in our search for the conditions in which personality may develop. Something has been said of good breeding, but as the highest beauty lies in expression, and the world soon tires of perfect features that lack it, so the long-solved material struggle does but prepare the ground by eliminating gross desires. We return to Proust's saying, and also remember that Becky Sharp climbed the social ladder to be ultimately bored. The soul uses the refined body to suggest a higher beauty ; for man seeks God in his fellow-creatures, and it was a doctrine of the neo-Platonists that a beautiful person could not be wicked. Hence are those stories eternally fascinating which tell how gods or angels have come down to live with men.

Thus the world labours to produce a race intermediate between God and man : the body on which generations of leisure have worked as with a chisel, the feelings— when not blasted by pride—responding to the sorrows of the lowest, the mind touched by those arts and philosophies which add thought to beauty. And to become a member of this race is the crown of all earthly effort, including art. Keats and Shelley were two of the most intense lyricists of all time, yet each laid aside his art before the close of his troubled life because the world would not listen. Surely this tribute of art to life proves that man's deepest desire is to be approved by man. And what exists scattered in the mass of men is brought to a focus in this selected intermediary race.

Each carries with him the memory of a human friend transfigured, and all moral codes and material considerations shrink to nothing by contrast with the immediate presence of man. He may be thought insincere, for he neither argues nor contradicts, never speaks a distasteful truth, promises what he cannot perform, and will discard a friend for an unlucky word. Yet through this over-value of mankind we see dimly on the outer edge of society something of heaven on earth, of the reign of love. But always the law holds good that heaven reveals itself through the earthly beauty of line and colour : and so we end where we began with Leonardo's saying of the smiling of women.

To the opinions of Carlyle and Proust which have been the props of this argument we now add a third. Professor Bradley described the tragic hero as intense rather than extraordinary—as one who thought and acted in a manner little removed from the average person but more energetically. We admire Antony and Cleopatra, for instance, and contemn the politic Octavius and his impeccable sister. The modern craving for personality has displaced the balance too far from mere good breeding to the region of despotic will and tempestuous passion. Never has the lot of undistinguished people been harder, nor the bore more severely let alone. In old days the human race was united by the subconscious thought of the brotherhood of man ; but now, in our eagerness to see the vision before the coming of night, we apply widely the mordant remark of Charles Maurras against literary egoists, that not everybody has a soul.

Having rejected the theory that an author's work is his best biography, but convinced that the writer of a great book has a great soul, and that to learn how this soul moved among us in its earthly vestments is to learn something of heaven, we pass on to glean what we can from Emily's books. And they also strike us, as did her life, by other-worldliness, by excess of soul over body. She has been called primitive, a descendant of giants and Titans, and so on, but this is not the emotion that *Wuthering Heights* conveys ; she is on the hither side of civilization, not before it begins but where it ends, and what Carlyle called the dim waste that lies beyond creation appears. The wild scenery of Wuthering Heights, the lonely moors impassable in winter, the stony track that leads off the main road to the deserted farm, where the slant of the stunted firs and thorns shows the force of the north wind, the rude furniture of the dwelling, the hard manners of its inmates—all point to something far withdrawn from the world we know. We are on the pinnacles of the moral world, with its restraints and conventions out of sight ; the scene is laid in a spot that has not changed since creation, and that symbolizes the end of civilization ; and there is nothing primitive in the souls of those who act out their destinies in these abandoned tracts. We can witness to this from our own experience of persons, the worst-mannered of whom we often find among the oldest European races, who have outlived their civilization, and care neither for art, chivalry nor the graces of life, but persist in money-making, as a last tie with their dying world.

As we approach the stern tale, something of at least the outlying parts of Emily's mind will be revealed. As common traits of the characters we may cite intellectual vigour and sarcastic speech, such as we might expect to find in the Yorkshire farmer or land-worker, out of whom Heathcliff was idealized : the effect of a keen brain and little education, solitude, hard weather, rough work. When old Mr. Earnshaw dies late at night, the messenger dispatched for the doctor and parson, returns with the doctor and says the parson will come in the morning. Heathcliff says sneeringly that Isabella Linton married him thinking he was a hero of romance, and at first none of his brutalities disgusted her. " I suppose we shall have plenty of lamentations now ! " exclaims Catherine when Edgar at last realizes the mortal nature of her illness. Catherine again is under no illusions as regards her lover ; she warns the infatuated Isabella that Heathcliff is a pitiless, wolfish man, not the kind who conceals depths of benevolence beneath a stern exterior. The above saying of Heathcliff leads to a further common trait of Emily's characters : their self-consciousness. Catherine speaks of turning her fits of frenzy to account ; Linton Heathcliff admits he has a bad nature and cannot be scorned enough, and is too mean for the younger Catherine's anger ; and many other instances spring to the mind. It is the trait which makes Shakespeare's characters psychologically real and individual : from Richard III, where it shows rather crudely, to the most consummate examples of his genius : Hamlet, Iago, Falstaff.

Like Shakespeare, Scott, Jane Austen, like all the most creative artists, Emily's characters become objective and self-moved ; the one point of contact with her personal nature is sarcasm. But it is a sarcasm bound up with intellectual vigour : the power to foresee clearly, while others, blinded by mere wishes, are dimly groping after truth. Keen untutored brains struggling with hard conditions might foster its growth in her models, but with Emily the cause was excess of spirit reacting on her own powerful mind, making this earth too small a point to see realized the thoughts she drew from the infinite. The note of Charlotte's writings is regret ; Charlotte would have been happy in a full family life, in society, in contact with any persons who treated her kindly. The tragedy of her life was enforced solitude ; whereas Emily, if she ever had worldly desires—and we gather from her poems that she had—conquered them once and for all. No doubt she grieved deeply at the immediate failure of *Wuthering Heights*, and she resigned further literary work, yet the fact remains that the balance is shifted too heavily on the side of soul for us to see her as a glorious earthly figure.

Charlotte describes nature as one who loves the joys

of this world ; the beauty of her landscapes in dawn or sunset is heightened by the suggestion from her own mind that another day has passed, and her hopes are unrealized, and death will come. Also, the love that she describes, though transcending time and space, is not entirely strange to earth. Most of us when first reading *Jane Eyre* in childhood knew that we were falsely told in the concluding chapter that Jane married Rochester ; we felt instinctively that the inner truth of the story was thereby violated, that the poor human institution of marriage was a small thing to two such souls wandering in eternity. And yet for a short spell they might have been happy on earth : Jane Eyre and Rochester at Thornhill, Lucy Snowe and Paul Emanuel in the schoolrooms of Villette. It is otherwise with Catherine and Heathcliff who, as children on the moors, had just a foothold in time, but cannot be imagined living together as man and wife even in the extra-conventional world of the story. But if their love is not of earth still less is it of heaven, and we must search for the true region where their souls have scope.

Many writers have attempted to depict a world beyond this, and none have succeeded like Emily. Haeckel, in the midst of foolish generalizations, did arrest our thought when he asked if we realized what we meant by eternity, and pointed to the profound legend of the Wandering Jew. Yet the desire to persist at least beyond this world is ineradicable, and Emily speaks in accents that convince us a further sphere exists. It comes to us in Mr. Lockwood's dream, and not Clarence's dream in *Richard III*, not the weird sisters in *Macbeth*, not the raising of Samuel by the Witch of Endor, have so true a ring of an actual experience of the soul. The keynote of the dream is subtly struck when sour old Joseph tells the younger Catherine that she will never mend her ways but go right to the devil like her mother before her. It is followed by the discovery of the writing in the old book which affects us strangely because we know that the writer has passed behind the veil. Then comes the dream : the tapping of the branch on the lattice ; the ice-cold hand which seizes the dreamer's ; the sobbing voice, " Let me in . . . I'm come home. I'd lost my way on the moor " ; the child's face looking through the window ; the reiterated cry, " It is twenty years . . . I've been a wait for twenty years " ; the effect on Heathcliff of sliding back the panels. . . .

What are the symbols that Emily uses so skilfully as to make us believe that this once-removed world exists ? In the first place we have the rude setting of the story, the point in life where all joyful social intercourse has ceased, and human relations are just preserved. It is neither primitive nor return to barbarism, but the end of a world, the dropping one by one of the refinements of life till the soul is naked. The austere moors, the bare dwellings typify it ; the coming of a stranger brings it home to us, like one of Shakespeare's underplots which reflect the main action and add a meaning. Such was Hindley Earnshaw's wife who came from no one knew where, without name or fortune, the " rush of a lass " far advanced in consumption, but who was so delighted with the old farm house that she would have nothing changed for her comfort, whose gay heart never failed her till within a week of her death. Catherine said well that she had no more right to marry Edgar Linton than to go to heaven, and her dream taught her how miserable she would have been in heaven. The Linton family does seem an alien presence on the moors, and the interior of Thrushcross Grange, into which Catherine and Heathcliff gaze spell-bound, with its crimson carpet and crimson-covered chairs and white and gold ceiling, so remote as almost to be unreal. Here again we see Emily's soul stronger than that of Charlotte, who described such things with a tinge of regret that she too did not live in splendid places and wear rich fabrics. Heathcliff's brutality is neither that of the savage, the boor, nor the over-civilized man driven mad, and it is truly imagined that he adds avarice to his other faults. When he strikes the younger Catherine he does the easiest thing to gain his object, because nothing else is worth while in a perishing world. The manner of his death typifies this world from which life is visibly receding. His son would be as cruel as he, but lacks the physical strength, and further proves that the material frame of things is crumbling before our eyes.

But if the soul is thus stripped naked, all the more urgent is its craving for love. It has attained the extreme point of earth, it reaches forward into the abyss beyond, it even exchanges messages with those whom the abyss has swallowed, and always it cries for love. Because of this we feel that the new world, a corner of which is mysteriously revealed, is more good than evil. That much evil remains—above all the sense of sin for earthly deeds—we do not dispute, but that love continues and will eventually triumph over sin, is the last conviction. Catherine's unrestrained childhood, the passionate dispositions of the Earnshaw family, Heathcliff's rough caresses which bruise the arm of his dying love—all these are symbols of the ultimate recovery of the spirit. Edgar Linton finds comfort in books after his wife's death, Hindley Earnshaw, in the same condition, becomes a gambler and raving drunkard. Because the soul is a real thing its conflict with gross matter is terrible : such was Hindley's unreasoning persecution of Heathcliff as a boy. While on earth it may appear worsted in its conflict with evil, but Emily has power to convince that the decision is elsewhere. The device of the Greek chorus has been a favourite one with playwright or novelist ; it here finds an unparalleled exponent in the character of Nelly Dean. Catherine confides her spiritual affinity with Heathcliff to be met with the retort : " If I can make any sense of your nonsense, Miss ———." As with Thersites in *Troilus and Cressida*, or Apemantus in *Timon*, her very blindness to the wonderland of Catherine's soul must flash some-

thing of its glory upon the dullest reader.   And always
the outer symbol of these storms of the mind is Wuthering
Heights itself, the mere shell of a home thrust away
from neighbourly kindnesses on its sterile promontory.

Turning from her novel to ask whether her poems will
supply the image of an earthly-heavenly creature, again
the answer is negative.   The balance may be shifted a
stage back towards earth, but is still not equal.   One
cannot but hear the cry of the heart in *Remembrance*,
but there is no means of knowing the proportion of real
and ideal.   Let us however recall a few of her best pieces
and brood over their distinctive charm.   Such are *The
Linnet*, *The Prisoner*, *The Lady to Her Guitar*, *How
Clear She Shines*, *Often Rebuked*, *The Outcast Mother*,
The Old Stoic, and the poem already mentioned.   Take
the last stanza of *The Linnet* :

> Blow, west wind, by the lonely mound,
>   And murmur, summer streams—
> There is no need of other sound
>   To soothe my lady's dreams.

And this from *The Lady to Her Guitar* :

> It is as if the glassy brook
>   Should image still its willows fair,
> Though years ago the woodman's stroke
>   Laid low in dust their Dryad-hair.

And place beside them these lines from Wordsworth's
Highland Reaper :

> A voice more thrilling ne'er was heard
> In springtime from the cuckoo bird,
> Breaking the silence of the seas
> Among the furthest Hebrides.

And this stanza of Mr. de la Mare's, the effect of snow
on fields at break of day :

> It hangs the frozen bough
> With flowers on which the night
> Wheeling her darkness through
> Scatters a starry light.

Differ as may the poet of fairy-land from the poet who, beginning with the beauty of nature, thereafter includes man, and so rises to believe in a divinely ordered universe, they are one in this : their vision of beauty has brought them peace on earth. It is not so with Emily who, though rivalling them in beauty, is at peace only with nature and not with man. The greatest poets carry with them an ideal world which is proof against intruders : thus William Blake, greater of course as mystic than poet, met and saluted the Apostle Paul in the Strand. Emily falls short of supreme greatness in that she is muted by a trespasser in her imaginative Eden. The earth must be delivered from man's presence before she can recognize it as Godlike ; she is inspired by night,— especially winter nights, when human activity is suspended for many long hours, or starry nights which suggest remote worlds where perhaps sin is not,—by the barest tracts of the moors where no house can resist the wind, by snow which muffles human footsteps and masks human traces, by time and death which defeat man, and make his mightiest happenings—his battles and empires, his material progress, the voices of orators, even the cry of sufferers—a momentary break in the eternal silence.

In this shrinking from her fellow-creatures, in their power to shatter her bright world by their mere presence, lay Emily's weakness. Yet she is stronger than Charlotte, who depended utterly on others, and whose consistent regret for lost happiness sounds in her every page. Had we biographical means to know whether this trait was inborn or developed by circumstances, much of the mystery of her personality would be solved. She confesses in her poems to a fleeting desire for fame, and such a stanza as this from *Remembrance* has an authentic ring :

> But when the days of golden dreams had perished,
> And even despair was powerless to destroy,
> Then did I learn how existence could be cherished,
> Strengthened and fed without the aid of joy.

But so have many of Shakespeare's sonnets, over which the battle between evenly-matched commentators has swayed backward and forward for generations. Suffice it that if from the internal evidence of her novel and poems we have realized more clearly what she was not, some slight advance has been made toward conceiving an image of her personality despite a forcedly agnostic conclusion.

" The Earthly Paradise "

" THE EARTHLY PARADISE "

IT was a cherished belief of childhood that the Garden of Eden still existed, that it would be possible to journey to the spot and approach as near as the beam of the fiery sword allowed ; perhaps even like Cain in Byron's tragedy to linger before the gates at twilight to catch a glimpse of the gardens. Great was the child's disillusion to learn that the Garden had long since vanished and only vague tradition pointed to the site. The belief was recalled by the saying of a British soldier in Mesopotamia during the Great War : that if this unpleasant place was Paradise, Adam and Eve were justified in committing any sin to escape from it. Something like these mental processes will appear in our appreciation of literature. The student brought up on the Classics and thinking their fame to be as strongly founded as the earth he treads on, will shudder at the first blast of what has been called Leslie Stephen's east wind. He will be told that something of the mildew of time is creeping over the Waverley Novels, that even Shakespeare had a message for his audiences which has not reached us, that out of a hundred books that have survived the centuries about ninety-nine have lost their freshness. We might supplement these statements by examples such as William Hayley, esteemed a great poet in his lifetime, now remembered by the accident that he was Cowper's friend. The three stages are thus made clear : what once appeared an enchanted domain is forbidden by the fiery sword of the critic ; and a latter-day public, typified by the sardonic soldier, denies that a Paradise existed.

From Leslie Stephen's favourite east wind we will take refuge in the milder climate of Pater. He instances from Gaston the special effect of contemporary poetry on sensitive youth, crystallizing the truant and irregular poetry of his own nature, and, because it was the latest achievement of the human soul in this matter, having the advantage of a personal presence. This brings us to our reason for selecting *The Earthly Paradise* as representing Morris at his best. Duly deferring to those critics who claim for *The Defence of Guenevere* a special charm which Morris never afterwards recaptured ; who are impressed by the mighty figures of *Sigurd ;* who discover some of his most beautiful work in *Poems by the Way*, we will none the less adhere to our choice. We will even better our instruction by eliminating the more elaborated second half, which includes *The Lovers of Gudrun*, and we will subdivide still further by selecting *Jason, The Prologue*, and the first four Greek stories only as expressing all that was good in Morris's nature. Time will prove the critics right, and our favourites may be the first to fall like ripe fruit, for only style can make the ship of song weatherproof as it sails the ocean of eternity, and these poems lack the final hardening touch. It behoves us all the more, while a gap of years still shows in the century since Morris was born, before the language has turned the corner, to remember Pater's saying and recapture in our souls some of the happiness overflowing from his. The western gate of Eden facing the sunset is still open and we can enter the blessed confine. Time may be when the critics will advance their fiery sword and forbid us all approach.

We will first note about Morris that, unlike the typical poet, he was well at ease upon earth. Life has been defined by biologists as the continuous adjustment of internal relations to external, and the same is true of mental life ; therefore to have imagination in excess hinders the mind from responding rhythmically to the fact. Perhaps the higher interest of a poet's life lies in this ill response : the unhappy marriage, the ruptured friendship, the wasted affection, the disappointed hopes ; and because Morris impressed his imagination to serve the fact, his life may lack this higher interest. However, we doubt not that he would rather have lived happily than have left a name to point a moral or adorn a tale ; and if he lived happily it was because he succeeded in externalizing his emotions. Only in his Homeric rages, and one other more notable thing to which we shall attend later, do we discover a personality transcending his daily occupations. He retained through life the friendships of his youth, and yet he is said not to have been an intense friend. The ugly Victorian age revolted him, but instead of merely lamenting, he founded a decorative art to bring beauty to the dwellings of the humblest. He felt keenly the injustice of the social order and the sufferings of the poor, and he became an active Socialist. He was a tremendous worker, often exceeding nine or ten hours a day in his task of weaving or dyeing or printing. His biographer observes that after his death the great difficulty was to realize his absence from the things which he had loved so well, " from his books and manuscripts, from his vats and looms, from the grey gabled house and the familiar fields." Even his poetic imagination was stayed by the mountains of Iceland ; and that he was more impressed by his second visit proves that his mind had not worked in the interval and produced vast shapes beyond reality, as would have been the case with poets like Shelley or Coleridge, the seed of whose imagination was in themselves. Only we note that at Kelmscott he took a solitary walk, wet or fine, when his day's work was concluded. Otherwise he was not a lonely man ; his mind did not make innumerable returns upon itself ; and with one exception he found things in the outer world to correspond with its movements.

An exception there was, for Morris was above all a poet, and he conquered the world by his imagination. He was haunted by the fear of death, and to this flight of the mind into a region beyond fact is due his greatest poetry. That we wish to escape death, and yet it is death which makes life sweet—this is the riddle he could not solve, as all his critics have pointed out. The worldly-busy man does not usually concern himself much with the thought of death ; the piers of his life-bridge are set firmly in the river bed of fact ; unlike him who walks the airy suspension bridge of art between birth and death. And yet even here, as we saw with his decorative and Socialistic efforts, the final result will be practical. There are means by which man becomes immortal in the flesh, and art is one ; but what is implicit in all art is explicit in the art of Morris. W. H. Hudson affirmed, in his delicate youth, that he could have forgotten the fear were he assured of at least another thirty years of life ; and he and others have remarked that such fears do not visit persons of strong body and active habits. Were it merely a matter of pursuing business or pleasure to forget the evil thought, we should gain little : hence the pathos of Dr. Johnson's saying that not one of the brilliant crowd whom he saw at Ranelagh would dare to go home and think. Our object is to be rid of fear, for fear prevents happiness, and happiness rightly used expands the soul : a happy man least fears death, as witness Othello's immortal words on landing at Cyprus. The past is beautiful because, as we look back upon our lives circle within circle, fear is withdrawn. It is otherwise with the unfilled circle of the present where the cares of the world prevent us from finding in beautiful earthly things symbols of heaven. We will endeavour to show how Morris used his art to make man conscious that he is immortal, and restore to him for a moment the finer life he lived in one of those completed circles of the past.

We selected as his most typical work *The Life and*

Death of Jason, originally intended to be part of *The Earthly Paradise, The Prologue* and the first four Greek stories : *Atalanta's Race, The Doom of King Acrisius, Cupid and Psyche,* and *The Love of Alcestis.* It is one of the literary paradoxes that such simple art, at so late an hour, should have captured the public ; for the public naturally suspects a late worker in simple things, and turns rather to the head of the centuries—to *The Canterbury Tales* or *The Faerie Queene*—for its narrative poetry. Morris worked no miracles with language— he deals in well-worn rhymes and metres—and his characters are but slightly individualized. He was no psychologist like Browning, no consummate jeweller like Tennyson, and he did not, like Swinburne or Baudelaire, so use the sound of words as to suggest the dream-emotions of the soul. The ebb of the romantic tide had long set in, and critics and prose-writers were at work upon the land reclaimed from the sea. Wordsworthians apologized for admiring *The Prelude* and *The Task,* and superior persons pronounced Byron's romances and *Childe Harold* affected, and only praised him as a satiric and therefore second-rate poet. The highest mood of the soul wrought in gold or ivory by the finest graving-tool of the artist became the law.

And yet Morris placed in the Temple of Art vessels of gold not wholly refined from ore, and the god received them. Let us briefly turn over the pages of our favourites and appreciate the emotion lying at their roots. In *Jason* it is the love of Jason and Medea—defining the conditions under which man holds his lease of happiness from the gods—that partly re-illumines a thrice-told tale. We do get effects characteristic of Morris that he will repeat more strongly in *Sigurd*—such as the flight of Argo through the Symplegades, or the stroke of her iron beak which splits asunder the ship of Absyrtus : it is when man sets the forces of nature to work and looks on wondering or trembling at the mighty recoil. But in the speech of Circe to Medea we see the soul of

Morris gleaming through the story's old brocade. That man may die without love makes even more remote that outer ocean which rings the world, into which Argo is driven, and more horrible the abyss down which her crew fear she may fall. It transforms Medea from a sorceress to a woman, and, when Jason betrays her, gives her the power to destroy her rival and even her own children.

Of *The Prologue* it may be said that the external adventures are not wholly subdued to the emotional tone. The two persist side by side, and the reader's attention oscillates between the vivid touches of mediæval imagery and the wistful spiritual refrain. Of the former we may cite the King with the falcon on his wrist and the scrivener to make notes for him ; the impenetrable woods on which axes scarcely make an impression, and where the vision of a dragon's head is hurriedly seen ; the need to await a breeze to land ; the mystery of what lies beyond the mountains ; the people who speak strange tongues ; the "crock of copper" and many another old-world phrase ; the strange pageant of armour and altars and barbarous customs—— All this is a means of escape for the spirit from our law-bound, exactly surveyed world, with its telegraphs amd steamboats, its smoke-blurred cities and the ravaged beauty of its countryside, and, worst of all, the ruined souls of its money-hunting inhabitants. And yet, when the deeper note is struck, it never fails to thrill through the reader's soul, and diminish the mere external adventures by contrast with the strange object of the quest. Witness the following lines where the Wanderers think they have attained the desired land :

> Old faces still reproached us : "We are gone,
> And ye are entering into bliss alone ;
> And can ye now forget ? Year passes year,
> And still ye live on joyous, free from fear ;
> But where are we ?——"

Atalanta's Race is one of the most beautiful of the stories, but even more than *Jason*, it is pictorially beautiful ; we delight more in the images that pass before our eyes than sorrow for the lost happiness of those who have failed in the race and fallen beneath the sword. Only we note how immediately Venus appears to Milanion in answer to his prayer—as a contrast to what has been called the inexorable silence of God in our modern world.

King Acrisius gives the same strange adventures as *The Prologue*, also inclining to the bizarre,—as the giants whom Perseus encounters upon the Libyan plain and overcomes with the Gorgon's head ; the same easy intercourse between God and man,—but we see the tide rising of that craving of the heart to become immortal on earth—which had driven the Wanderers forth—now applied to the master-subject of these stories—love. It begins with Danaë's lament as she wanders through the chambers of the brazen tower, and grows more intense when she herself is immured there. It is the homesickness of those who have lost the world and did not suspect how beautiful it was. But when Perseus woos Andromeda upon the shore, we return to the mood of Jason and Medea : how love alone can create in the individual heart that new world which the Wanderers have vainly sought over so many seas.

If the interest in *The Prologue* and *King Acrisius* is dual, this defect—if defect it is—is remedied in *Cupid and Psyche*. All the beauties of the piece are disposed in circles round the heart-hunger of the central figure. We may even wonder that Cupid seeks for his beloved a godlike immortality, for this earth is so dressed as to appear a true pattern of heaven. As the narrative proceeds the emotion becomes acuter, and Psyche as a bride is less lovely than Psyche seeking her lost love. and enduring the tasks of the angry Venus. Her journey to the underworld will recur to us later, but meanwhile we note that the story expands into the culminating effort of Morris's art, *The Love of Alcestis*. Here not only do the gods hear the prayers of man and accept his sacrifices, but live with him as a brother or comrade ; they aid him to attain love on earth, and would give him immortal life if they could. Morris's genius culminates in this piece, for it completes what *The Prologue* began. That which the Wanderers set out to seek is here made the subject of the story ; the two streams meet, and henceforth they part. The reader knows he can approach no nearer to the heart of the mystery, and his interest declines.

For it must be remembered that the setting of the tales is as important as the tales themselves, and as we listen we must keep in mind's eye the Elders and Wanderers who tell them. Be it remembered also that the stories are told, not read, and we should endeavour to hear the voice and its changes as the images pass before us. And the subjects are related to the grand adventure in the lives of these Wanderers or modern Argonauts : their quest after another and still fairer Golden Fleece. Not only they, but men in all ages, because this earth is beautiful, have wished to be at home on it for ever, or to attain that state of mind where they believe that such things can be. Only love can bring it to a man alone, but to the Wanderers no longer young, and travel-weary, companionship can still do something : as we know from the cruder instance of those whom Dr. Johnson pitied. Each as a solitary might smile incredibly and indulge in Hamlet-like musings, but among his fellows, amid the flowing tides of rhythm, and with golden fancies passing before the mind's eye, he is immortal and divine.

And this emotion, not confined to the page but overflowing it, is the distinctive one of *The Earthly Paradise*. We are conscious of the magic circle of Elders and Wanderers with the wonderlight in their eyes, and we reflect that we too have our friends and would like to share this happiness with them. The lyric poet is best read in solitude ; and it is only thus that we can admire to the full the Virgilian diction of Tennyson, or the miracles worked in rhyme and metre by Swinburne, and catch the last echoes of their harmonies in our remoter mind. Or if we speak of them it is to quote selected passages, which we rarely do with *The Earthly Paradise.* With these stories it is the whole that concerns, not necessarily in the poet's own words but in the emotion they give off. They were spoken to an audience, and the effect is as when we gaze into one of two opposing mirrors, and see our own image in a receding line, till reflections of reflections dwindle to nothing in the long perspective. We all carry with us an imaginary world of Elders and Wanderers to whom we long to confide the good news of a younger world when gods lived with men. Morris has made this world real to us, and the distinction is that when we speak of it or explain it to others, it does not lose its magic as beautiful things do when exposed to the light of day. The emotion is an artistic-social one which grows with telling.

If we read these stories singly, apart from their framework, we miss their essential purpose. Other poets have surpassed Morris as story tellers ; he has added nothing new to familiar legends ; and he has not adorned Greek art like Keats or Tennyson or Swinburne. And yet, even though it has been pointed out that he is more mediæval than Greek in spirit, the emotion is due to the beauty which we distinctively associate with ancient Greece. The familiar names of the gods, the genial climate, the islands, the blue seas, the white temples, pass before our eyes and contrast with our hideous modern life. Thus, having fixed the mood by striking the old chord in the memory, Morris compels us to accept collectively what singly we might not do—the imaginative truth of his stories. We gaze at the rapt faces of his circle, we know the thoughts of his listeners—that they yearn, as all men do, for the return of a golden age, for a simpler and more beautiful world where gods lived with men—in fact, to be immortal here on earth.

And this emotion, that rather glides from the surface of the mind if experienced in solitude, finds its way to the deep places when shared with others. Instead of growing thinner, as emotion does when spoken of, it is heightened by exchange with other minds : and this power of endlessly reproducing their own images is peculiar in poetry to these few stories. From watching the effect imaginatively on the Elders and Wanderers, we long to tell our own living circle how such things chanced in Morris's ideal world. We wish other minds to work on scenes as where the kind god pitied Admetus because he had to die,—and when he left Pherae something of his spirit remained with Admetus, so that men thought the golden age had come again,—and when Admetus summoned him to his deathbed he appeared, not like a god, but in the same dress as when he kept the herds, wearing the same homespun coat and carrying the bow in his hand and the quiver slung over his shoulder. Or how Psyche in the hall of Proserpine felt the spell of death around her and doubted whether she cared to return for a few short years to the living world, till the goddess warned her to take the casket and begone because her eyes were growing strange.

When *The Love of Alcestis* is concluded, the peak of beauty is passed, and the reader travels downward regretting much that has gone before. The stories interleaved between the first four Greek stories gain something from their position : like the Falstaff scenes in *Henry IV* they rest the reader's mind amid the great national happenings of the play. But with *Alcestis* the two streams meet, and thenceforth they part, so that the reader is alone with the stories that follow. The social virtue of their predecessors has gone out of them, and the reader, as he follows the stream of narrative, no longer hears the comments of those who sail what was the companion *Prologue* stream, which has now meandered miles away over the forsaken country. This is not to reflect on the stories themselves, that have been praised by some critics above the earlier ones. There is a pathos, so far not attained, in *The Land East of the Sun and West of the Moon*. Aslaug, in the story that bears her name, is a more vivid individual figure—but she is alone in her world. And such a lonely world is that of the greatest of all, where Morris's epic manner begins : *The Lovers of Gudrun*. There indeed we see a human heart isolated in a land of rocks, surrounded by the untaught, and divided from civilization by green wintry seas, so that love is the one relief. Hence the reader hopes that love may be enjoyed, and as the temptation to break plighted troth looms darkly, his fears grow tense with agony, and he foresees the inevitable wreck of happiness and life.

From *Gudrun* dropped the seed that took root in good soil and bore fruit a hundred fold in *Sigurd ;* but this work has been extravagantly praised of late years. It elevates human beings through the natural scenes in which their lot is cast, but fails in cumulative interest because the centre of interest is not the individual and not wholly his actions, but rather the circumstances under which actions are performed. The stupendous scenes exalt the persons into fellowship with them, so that the work of their hands is fitly compared to fire or frost or thunder. The interest ebbs and flows according as they engage in adventures which suggest likenesses with the roll of the seasons or the features of a land untimely ripped from chaos. The white sword of Sigurd is " still as the moon," and the throne of King Gripir " a chair of the sea-beast's tooth." So huge are the mountains that " the floor of heaven was mingled with the tossing world of stone."

This last line gives us pause, and we have already

noted that Morris was more impressed by his second visit to Iceland. Compare these lines of Milton :

> Beyond this flood a frozen continent
> Lies dark and wild, beat with perpetual storm
> Of whirlwind and dire hail.

And now consider another of Morris's lines, from a passage describing the precipices of a distant mountain range :

> And lower yet are the hollows striped down by the scanty green.

From this and the above line we deduce that Morris actually saw such sights in Iceland and retained them in his memory ; and that his mind had not wandered from the time he saw the object to the time he recorded it in verse ; whereas Milton's lines refer to no one thing, but are compounded of many effects, seen and read of, unconsciously refined through years of reverie and dream. And while Milton gave his whole life to *Paradise Lost*, Morris composed *Sigurd* in little more than a year.

We have dwelt upon *Sigurd* because it illustrates most clearly that Morris worked with his memory, and that out of his memory he gave us what is sublime in *Sigurd* and wistful in *The Earthly Paradise*. Critics have observed that his imagination was homesick for another age, and in his youth he took refuge in Mediævalism from the hideous world about him. In later years he visited Iceland, and that satisfied his craving for external beauty on the grander scale, so that he reproduced it as it was. But from the earlier spiritually-realized life of the Middle Ages sprang the peculiar emotion of *The Earthly Paradise* that does not fade when it is spoken of. When old friends meet they speak of the past, and memories that were growing faint in the individual live again, and the more there are to share them, the more objectively real do they seem. Memory,

like art, is concrete, and sharers of a common past suggest
the emotion by recalling the time worn things of home
and small material accidents—we noted how the god
reappeared garbed as a herdsman—till the half faith
of each member of the circle produces a whole faith,
while the circle endures, in that earthly-heavenly immortality which love and friends and art and beautiful
houses and gardens, and dawn and sunset, and the
seasons, promise to man in health but withdraw in
sickness.

For all its splendour, *Sigurd* is like a literary exercise
because the emotions were felt by the mature man and
reproduced by the perfected craftsman ; they had not
grown with his growth and reached back to an idyllic
past, as did those of *The Earthly Paradise* to the days
of childhood when he rode about Epping Forest in
toy armour and fancied himself a knight errant.   The
basis of poetry is refined emotion, and as Morris, unlike
most poets, could externalize his emotions and dwell
much at ease on earth, his art suffered, for the mind
needs two recoils from fact.   *Sigurd* marks one recoil,
the chosen stories of *The Earthly Paradise* that second
and further recoil into the land of memory.   For
memory visited the shores of Morris like the Gulf
Stream, and made genial weather in a northern
clime.

We do wrong to regard life as a material thing, for man,
while on earth, is a spirit, and already half immortal.
He has never accepted the argument that we do wrong
to knit human ties too closely because death will rend
them, nor consoled himself for misfortune by reflecting
that in a hundred years he and all about him will have
quitted the stage.   When himself about to die, his
thoughts are still busy with the affairs of this world, not
the next ; and when his nearest die, he grieves like
fallen Lucifer.   The past is the only heaven he knows,
and for this reason, bereaved persons do well to seclude
themselves from the world, because those who feel the

taint of mortality are not fit companions for immortals.
But when he loves, or finds a friend, or reads the written
words, or surveys the painted canvas, or hears the
musical strains, of a master, he becomes wholly immortal in the present. Morris has achieved this effect
by uniting art and love and friendship more consciously
than other writers ; and his lines gain in beauty as they
pass from mind to mind. The mountains of his horizon
look blue some scores of miles nearer than those which
only distance glorifies. He has given the soul a double
reminder—to use the old Platonic phrase—of its pre-
natal home. And mental progress—despite the Freu-
dians—consists in working the broken tracks on the
unconscious mind into straight Roman roads.

And so because Cupid loved Psyche, and Apollo was
tender with Admetus, we feel, as we read or even explain,
a stronger link with our own friend or beloved, and the
emotion returns with tidal rhythm—through the intermediary listening circle—to heighten our interest in the
story. But Aslaug and Gudrun and Rhodope are lonely
women, for though their fortunes move us, we turn the
page and forget. For after the Watersmeet of *Alcestis*
the two streams diverge, and despite the exquisite
linking stanzas, the voices on the narrative stream
scarcely carry to *The Prologue* stream. The country has
grown bleaker, and here again is the obstinately recurring
simile of Mesopotamia, the seat of Paradise, with which
our inquiry opened. But if we shrink from attempting
the bleaker country, let it not be thought that we wish
to anticipate future generations and unbuild our Paradise. No : we will yet linger on the banks of the two
streams, like those in Morris's own magical song :

> Drawn from the purple hills afar,
> Drawn down unto the restless sea.

We cannot withdraw the former caution that these
stories may be defeated of their immortality through
lack of the firmest art-control ; but we will thankfully

note that Morris, who lived a happy life, was happy in the end, for the fear left him as it did Dr. Johnson at the last. It was Jowett who once wrote beautifully, that Nature, like a kind nurse or mother, puts us to sleep without frightening us.

The Heart of the Wessex Novels

THE HEART OF THE WESSEX NOVELS

THE latest movements of Hardy in the world of letters have diverted public attention from those which first brought him fame. Readers preoccupied with the *Dynasts* and the various collections of poems, run the risk of forgetting the message of beauty which he first delivered. Confronted with Hardy's formal creed of pessimism, we need to remind ourselves that it is the artist's duty to suggest rather than assert,— that the thought which the brain conceives must pass through his soul before it can reach the world, and that many a true artist—like him of whom we speak— will convert, at the eleventh hour, and like Balaam in spite of himself, his curse to a blessing.

It will therefore not be amiss to restate the beauties of the Wessex novels, since it is on a basis of beauty that Hardy's philosophy and so-called pessimism have been built. The greatest living national master of fiction, he stands in the direct line reaching back through Meredith to George Eliot, and thence through Dickens, Thackeray, and the Brontës, to Scott and Jane Austen, and, further still, through Goldsmith, to Fielding and Smollett, Richardson and Defoe, the creators of the modern novel. The sound of these names recalls to the reader a special manner or grand characteristic : how wide apart is the satire of Fielding and Jane Austen, the passion of George Eliot and Charlotte Brontë ! Hardy's great achievement is having carried to a successful conclusion the revolution initiated by the Brontës : he has transformed the content of the novel from prose to poetry. There have been poetical novels before his time, but not novels which are poems. In *Wuthering Heights* and portions of *Jane Eyre*, the novel so far exceeded its primal objects of portraying character or manners or telling a story, as to produce in the reader a strange emotion from interacting characters and scenes. But even in the first of these two books there was much to be contributed by the reader from his common experience with the author. Hardy has gone a stage further from the real world and subjected his readers to a definite vision, differing from his predecessors as the prose writer who uses words and relies on their total approximate effect from association of ideas, differs from the poet who mobilises to the full the resources of every word.

The territories created by the great masters enumerated, like Cæsar's gardens, have been bequeathed to the whole population, and at all hours of the day we may walk in them and recreate ourselves. But Cæsar's gardens were on this side Tiber, whereas the paler lands of Hardy lie beyond to the far horizon, and are best seen from a distance by eyes into which the three magic drops have been distilled. Something of the poetic meditation which has gone to make them must be renewed by a truly appreciative reader. How the outer world has gradually receded in literature we may judge from the very greatest. When Achilles speeds across the plain against Troy, he appears " blazing as the star that cometh forth at harvest time." When Claudio ponders the destiny of the soul, he imagines a " thrilling region of thick-ribbed ice." In Homer the images are more like parallel rivers of thought than tributaries of the main stream : in Shakespeare they are directly produced by the mental agony. In Homer they exist independently of the mind, to recall to the reader that beautiful world of sense which justified the outer existence of the Greek.

The modern imaginative writer, then, does not venture out into the world, but resembles a dweller in those mountain caves each of which leads back to another, so that no man may discover their end. If his voice is inward that of his successor will be more so, as he retreats further into the bowels of the mountain. Or, to change the metaphor, as gold will not coin without alloy, so did his thought once require an admixture of sensible objects known to the thought of others ; but every generation reduces the measure of alloy, till we now see him struggling in solitude to shape the pure gold of his idea.

To say that the half-dozen greater novels of Hardy are far from the real world, and that he does not help us to recreate his characters by appealing to a common stock of experience, is not intended to deny their truth to life. The most real thing is emotion, and the effect of the Wessex novels is to kindle a particular emotion. They are like a dream which, when its outer events are forgotten, lingers in the form of emotion surpassing in haunting-power that of our waking hours : more especially when it revives memories of a happy past in days of present sorrow. For when man's bodily activities are suspended, his soul recovers its gigantic power to experience, and, troubled in its mortal foldings, is made home-sick for a perfection that cannot be attained on earth. Hardy's vision of beauty is therefore a dream, the emotion from which is stronger than that thrown off from his waking hours of pessimism.

But as there are dreams of more or less beauty, so it is with the Wessex novels, and our object is to appreciate in them those qualities which exalt them to the perfect dream world, and reject foreign elements which debase them to waking life. Judging by this standard, we would give first place to the *Return of the Native*, which, though eclipsed in parts by *Tess* and *Jude*, best follows the course of an unbroken dream, and leaves behind a more single emotion. It is eclipsed by parts of *Tess* because its prevailing tone is sombre, and Hardy is at his best when describing the joy of life, no matter how soon to disappear,—but it surpasses as an artistic whole. Its great catastrophe, the death of Mrs. Yeobright, affects the reader to its full, without wrenching the fabric of the story like the death of Tess. The world presented is the ancient one where all memories are centred in earth, the common mother, and all characters modified thereby, but the joys of innocence are gone. The outer world, built by the deliberate design of self-conscious man, exists, but it does not do violence to the structure like the characters of Alec d'Urberville or Edred Fitzpiers. It is emotionally present in the mind of Eustacia Vye isolated on Egdon Heath, making Budmouth seem a Paradise to her, and a man from Paris like a messenger from heaven. Its pool-like shallowness compared to the ocean-depth of inherited memories and customs is exemplified in Clym Yeobright who, on his return, easily throws off the veneer of modern cities. But it is the heath itself which refines and exalts the emotion by the previous effect upon the character of its vast dark spaces unresponsive to the moonlight, its loneliness, its steadfastness, its great age. It is finely imagined that Clym, when nearly blind, should retire to Alderworth, and another dark stretch of the unknown be opened up. It extends the mystery of the heath into remoter circles of dreamland, and gives to the episode of the furze-cutting, with the visit of Mrs. Yeobright in the torrid heat of afternoon, the effect of a dream within a dream. But although the sounds from the outer world are not loud enough to break the magic ring of sleep, they suffice to make the sleeper turn uneasily. For, as a child may have a sudden foreboding of the cares and sorrows of age and the coming of death, so did nature, when the world was young, fashion these swarthy monotonies against times that should no longer be fair. Solitude, despair, brooding melancholy, are the human moods which the heath reflects, and intensifies by its interaction with character, so that we must look further for the full unfolding of Hardy's powers.

Under primitive conditions, before the days of town life and education, Hardy maintains there was an appetite for joy and zest for existence. If man had been content to draw his daily sustenance from nature and spend his leisure in communion with her, he would have remained happy : but he preferred to snatch at what he thought a higher knowledge, to think of the future, to abandon nature for man, to create conventions and an artificial way of thinking. These are the clouds that appear singly or mass thickly upon the skies of *Tess*,— otherwise the fairest in the world of fiction. The *Native*, though a faultless dream, was never many fathoms below the waking level, and its beauty was shot through with cares assimilated from the outer world. *Tess* is composed of separate dreams, and though they are broken up by discordant sounds, while they endure their beauty is of the kind that suspends hell and ravishes the thronging audience. It is a beauty created by Hardy's sympathy with all that is good in the peasant's life and character, refined by its passage through the soul of one who, while preserving unchanged his earliest love for the earth, has travelled far mentally and explored the thought and literature of many countries and ages. To him knowledge has not brought distaste for primitive pleasures and scorn for unlettered people : it has made his love greater by making his sensibilities more exquisite. It is in his agnosticism—common to the leading minds of the last half of the nineteenth century—that we find the disharmony. For the Christian idea, and the conception of this world as a transitory place, is not one that can be discharged from the subconscious mind. Hence we feel the hand falter as it depicts the pagan pleasures of the villagers and their self-adoration. Like the fears of the brave and follies of the wise, there is the home-sickness of the advanced mind that will not conceive of this world as the pattern of a diviner one.

Therefore, except in rarest moments, when the blending of earth and seasons and human emotions fulfils the reader's vision, there is joy on a basis of apprehension. The green and golden fields, the old forest trees with Druidical mistletoe, the azure landscapes, are beautiful but lonely in their beauty. A time may come when the human mind, preoccupied with the future and enslaved by social conventions, will turn from them even more completely than it does now. Thus the impression grows that the days of joy are numbered, the shadow is growing, and the beauty of earth may perish like the physical beauty overrun by thought.

In *Tess* we hear every stop sounded of that complex modern instrument of thought and emotion. We experience the deepest dream of all where joy prevails unchecked, we traverse the middle region of joy on a basis of apprehension, and we are summoned to the outer world by sounds of terrifying discord.

In the *Native* the dream was unbroken though less deep because its sombre background remembered an outer world no longer fair : less deep than in parts of *Tess* where the sun and moon stand still in some Ajalon of the human spirit. The world of Jude is outside the dream, but the memory of it is the charm of the book. If Jude and Sue behave imprudently in the real world of to-day, it is because they belong to the ideal past and import some of its beauty into the sordid present. The dream-world, because it is immaterial, is not shattered from contact with the real, but sheds some of its glory on the endless straight roads and mean figures that hurry down them. The light of their spirits is strong enough to form a radiant cloud in which they move, isolated in populous ways, and at times is dazzling enough to transfigure the unlovely street into mountainous solitudes. Like Christian and Faithful in the town of Vanity, their meek, joyful bearing converts enemies to friends. If the catastrophe, awful as in *Tess*, is yet in keeping, which that of *Tess* is not, it is because the book is founded on a definite code of manners. The two escaped figures from the dream-world eventually succumb, but the wreck is of the body rather than the soul.

It would be possible to trace Hardy's golden legend in the more ideal scenes of his other greater novels—such as the episode of Fanny Robin in *Far from the Madding Crowd*, or all that concerns Marty South in the *Woodlanders*—or to watch its fainter appearance in the books that stand just behind the inner circle, or even its dawn in his earliest essays in fiction. But for the present we prefer to stand at the centre and ask ourselves what is his basis of reality without which no work of art can endure ? Where is the ladder planted on solid earth yet reaching to the heaven of his dreams ?

And we find this basis in the soul of the peasant, because the peasant, thus idealized, is distinguished with one other class still surviving in corners of the world, by possessing a soul. This other class is made up of those members of the old aristocracy who are not infected by the modern desire for wealth. Of these two—the true peasantry and the true aristocracy—it is only the first who can embody Bacon's maxim and despise riches because they despair of them,—whereas the second, used through long centuries to material possessions, walk easily beneath their burden, converting it to an adornment which does not hide the graces of nature or become an armour plate to obscure the light of the soul. Between these poles of society revolve the socialistic artisan class, and the many circles of the money-getting bourgeois class,—who take thought for the morrow and sacrifice present to future, who condemn vice because it is expensive or may cause a scandal, who make marriages like contracts in business, whose ideals are respectability and material efficiency, in pursuit of which they encrust themselves more and more stiffly with the mud of this planet.

We know that deceit lies in generalities, and that any-one could immediately confute this theory with a dozen instances from his own experience. It is just as true, according to the naturalistic French novels, that there are some peasants distinguished by a ferocious love of money —as also that there are members even of the old aristoc-racy with human sympathies atrophied by care for rank and position. We must also except the intellectual classes, in whom the practice of art should stimulate the working of the spirit. But it has been said that generali-ties are necessary, and it therefore remains roughly true that the unsophisticated soul is most often found in the peasant and the nobleman,—in those who are above competition and those who decline it.

And as art is concrete, and it is the artist's duty to interpret ideally the facts of his experience, so are these two classes who enshrine what beauty is left in the distracted modern world, fittest for his treatment. In the one we have the beauty evolved by centuries of cul-ture, education, easy living : beauty of face and form, of speech and manner, of that kind of disinterested thought which is the offspring of leisure. In the second —and here Hardy is our best guide—we have the beauty of the simple man directly associated with nature. Just as he owes to her his moral characteristics—his generosity, his loyalty, his freedom from suspicion—so is his out-ward form exalted by sharing in her moods. We see him empurpled by the sunset, one with the brown heath or green of the meadows, a very brother to autumn, interpreter of the language and music of the trees. . . .

The theme of Hardy's novels is to make visible the beauty of these souls, whether in their native places, or in their interaction with the world, which, though it rejects them as false prophets, by contrast with its own darkness, bears witness to their light. But it is in the first of these endeavours that Hardy's art becomes perfect, that we detect in him something of a Renaissance mood : for it is a fact of the individual mind, as of the embryo, that it repeats the experience of the race. The distinctive trait of the Renaissance was its morning freshness, despite the use made of classical models to further its own artistic expression. But in the long interval between ancient and mediæval art, the soul had grown strong in silent meditation, and when the seal of the cloister was broken, it reshaped old forms and transfigured old themes with its terrific stored energy. Not only in art but in life did the spiritual triumph over the material,—did human beings judge each other not by the accident of outward form or worldly station, but the intrinsic beauty of the soul : as we know from the sonnets of Shakespeare and many others, it was the fashion for men to address each other in the language of love. Granted that this spiritual loosening comes to the individual as to the race, we understand how Hardy, who was not born in an age of faith, himself agnostic, scholar, philosopher, should, while flashing the lamp of knowledge down the shaft of his soul, dis- cover in its lowest depth—in the simplest type of human being—the most fitting material for his genius.

It is no mere sentimental Rousseau doctrine of return to nature to remedy the ills of civilization, that Hardy preaches. He chooses the peasant's lot because there is something in the prior inherited experience of his soul which the spiritual loosening caused by the impact of his Renaissance wave has brought to the surface. And as in the Renaissance proper old forms were pressed into the service of new ideas, so does the highly evolved brain of the artist, the scholar's learning, the sceptic's melan- choly, make more poignant the fate of those who fulfil the oldest tasks in the world. In the morning freshness of the Renaissance the soul awoke from its thousand years of reverie, and man went forth to enjoy the present on earth, eager as a child who is not haunted by a happier past, but with the faculties of mature age. The centre of the emotion we receive from Hardy is, therefore, pure joy,—as witness those of his pictures which dwell longest in our minds : Tess who would make of her love a long betrothal, and who—like Thomasin Yeobright—scarcely understands angry words from one she loves, only recognizing anger by its sound ; Jude and Sue who walk through life wrapped in the cloud of their love, unconscious of a jeering world ; Clym Yeobright—to a lesser extent because the dream is less deep—so far forgetting his lost ambition that he can sing while cutting furze on the heath, to the despair of his wife. These are the moments when man becomes as if immortal on earth, for the great emotions, like the great passions of which Coleridge spoke, are atheists believing in no future.

But the white light which forms the centre of the emotion is surrounded by darker rings. If the men of the Renaissance believed in an earthly paradise, they were unconsciously buoyed up by an accumulated spiritual reserve. The centuries that followed saw the slow wasting of this reserve, and though the individual may re-duplicate the Renaissance mood, the roots of his being do not strike down to the vast underground circulation of spiritual waters. In the eighteenth century was born that modern scientific, utilitarian world, which the professional and business and artisan classes who have come to control it, look upon as a real thing, not a symbol of a diviner world. Man, it has been said, is born brother of his contemporaries, and therefore the two nigh extinct classes who conserve humanity's best gift, are often repudiated both by God and their fellow-creatures. They have neither the strength to force their way through life, nor the faith which makes its triumphs or defeats seem but a little thing.

The emotion felt by the sonneteer of the Renaissance was a religious one, because he saw God manifested in the soul of his friend or mistress : and the summit of religion is to prefer good to evil simply because God wishes it so. This exalting of the Person and neglect of mere moral maxims and prudential restraints is also the point of union between saint and artist, but in ages of little faith, when communications between earth and heaven have grown intermittent, it has peculiar dangers. For the elect soul of to-day, though also prompted to worship God in human shape, fails to see when beauty of outward form loses its true character of index to beauty of mind, and, retaining its native instinct to accept as law the wish of the beloved,—too gentle to contradict, and unfortified by bourgeois morality and suspicion,— is beckoned down to the low places. The sons of God become entangled with the daughters of men.

Thus in Hardy's pages we see Tess momentarily dazzled by Alec d'Urberville, Jude sacrificed to Arabella, Fanny Robin abandoned by the world. Yet to record the misadventures of chosen spirits born out of their due time would describe inadequately the emotion we receive from Hardy. It is but partial truth that he is a pessimist, for these rubs and crosses and mischances which wreck human lives are but outward constraints imposed upon the soul : the mere bolts and bars which prison it in its earthly house. The light we see burning within admonishes us that its native faculty to enjoy remains unquenched. As the Phœnician merchants who lit a fire in sand and saw a wondrous film forming were the first to discover glass,—so, as we labour in the desert places, there rises before us a magic window through which glimmers for a moment an enchanting landscape.

In the grief of those who lose all that makes life sweet, or even life itself, we find unexpected evidence that somewhere or other this happiness exists : in the lost Paradises, of love with Tess or Marty South, of learning with Jude. The words written with chalk on the pauper coffin, " Fanny Robin and child," raise a picture of the sheltered life of love that should have been the lot of such a beautiful-minded being. The effect is not wholly one of contrast, nor a further example of Dante's divine saying ; it rather resembles the coming of faith at the eleventh hour to the troubled soul. And this final emotion shows clearest in the story, *To Please his Wife,*—the best of Hardy's short stories, and one of the best in the world—because instances crowd thick and fast within the smallest space. What infinite suggestion is there in the three visionary forms which the bereaved wife and mother sees kneeling every Sunday on the chancel-step ! (They recall the words of the witness, how three men were cast into the furnace, but four might be seen walking unharmed amid the flames.) Does not the eternally level waste of waters southward, unbroken by the longed-for mainmast, tell of a sea in some other world that will not bear our friends away ? Do not the actual ravages of grief—the greyed hair, the lined forehead, the gaunt and stooping form—hint at a more ideal beauty ? How fair must have been the lost thing that could awaken such regret ! . . . At the lowest deep there is a sudden turn of Fortune's wheel, and we are in a world of reversed laws,—where fire does not burn, nor water drown,—where on days of hazy calm and sea like glass, ships seem to be sailing in the heavens.

But speculation may lead too far, and as we soar upward amid clouds of fancy, the silken thread which unites body and spirit may snap, and the dreamer awake no more. Let us therefore conclude by bringing before the mind's eye some of those pictures where earth and heaven are one. We will think of Clym Yeobright at work on Egdon Heath, and almost subdued to its colour, while the strange amber-coloured butterflies quiver in the breath of his lips, alight upon his bowed back, and sport with the glittering point of his hook ;—of the pink flowers reflected in Sue's pale cheeks as she bends towards them ;—of Fanny Robin whose first question on waking from her swoon in the portals of Casterbridge Workhouse is for the dog without whose assistance she would not have reached that dreadful haven ;—of Tess returning from her first visit to Alec d'Urberville,—roses at her breast, roses in her hat, roses and strawberries in her basket to the brim.

Swinburne

SWINBURNE

THE once popular conception of Swinburne as a poetic innovator has disappeared, and we regard him rather as the latest representative of the great race of poets descended from Chaucer. Without wishing to cast a stone at the bards of contemporary England, it may be asserted that their abandonment of the grand tradition marks a definite break in the evolution of their art. That not the quality of individual genius but the late hour of civilization in which these singers have appeared on earth, is at fault, we do not dispute : but our wonder is increased tenfold at the man who, coming late among a jaded audience, has yet charmed it with sweet sounds that recall its youth.

As the centuries lengthen the anthology will play an increasingly important part ; and we are reminded that not the Xerxes' hosts but the handful of Marathon march on to immortality. And as the ancient moralist forbade any man to be called happy till he were dead, so we may deny a poet assured fame till his language has ceased to be a living force. For poetry (like all things) is in a condition of advance towards its goal of perfect speech ; the poetry of one generation may become the prose of the next, and the fame of the individual perish as in some Tarpeian tragedy, or by self-immolation through the general advance in beauty of a language of which he was at first the pioneer. We must grant therefore that only a small portion of a poet's output is known as poetry to the fourth generation, though its vital force may preserve from decay a huge uninspired main body. In order to estimate Swinburne's peculiar contribution to a literature already overflowing with riches, it behoves us to attempt some description of the art of poetry,—and we use the word description rather than definition, knowing how often the latter has been tried in vain.

Poetry, we may say in metaphor, is the speech of angels, based upon the emotion of love which rules their spiritual world,—unlike the logic-bound speech of man. The poet, wandering far from his fellows, ascends the mountain, and, if his strength fail not, draws near the summit. The exhilarating quality of the air intoxicates him ; the law of gravitation ceases to act ; he rises as on wings towards the gates of heaven and overhears some strains of the celestial music. These, in his great joy, he translates into earthly symbols and gives to the lower world, and is henceforth honoured as one inspired. But, as time passes on, his exquisite phrases grow familiar to man, are vulgarized by repetition, and at last even refused the title of poetry in a language which they have helped to enrich.

For the snatches of divine song thus overheard are transcribed by the poet in an alien tongue. Even as he meditates over his experience it fades like the beauty of a dream. There is thus no equality among those admitted to the beatific vision ; all depends on the fineness of the instrument with which he reaches from earth to heaven : his individual heart and brain. And if these in some cases obscure the divine message, in others fling only a temporary splendour upon the page, and in a few kindle unextinguished lamps in the corridor of this lower world,—it is the critic's duty to explain the causes. Having, therefore, established in our minds an approximate idea of poetry in the abstract, we proceed to an examination of the poet's soul.

The leading characteristic of Swinburne's nature was its healthiness : though this may seem a strange statement in view of the stories of dissipations, etc., connected with his name. But we learn from the pages of Sir Edmund Gosse that his fevered London life was based upon an inherited fund of healthiness,— as proved by the magical recoveries which he made on his return to the country. His birth in 1837 coincided with the formal outbreak of the unlovely Victorian age. It was a time when the professional and business classes were refusing pleasure and knowledge for the sake of money : a form of asceticism compared by Ruskin to the two others which have possessed the world—the religious and military. Its most sinister commandment against rightful enjoyment for children was to lead in the third generation to widespread moral and nervous disaster, and the projection of many who escaped madness or early death into careers of heartless ambition or grovelling sensuality : thus vindicating the Aeschylean doctrine that sin entails suffering upon the innocent. Swinburne's ancestors were those who had devoted themselves to the public services and given their best for the sake of honour rather than profit, so that thanks to his family's high social position, in a world still safe from democracy, his childhood was of the happiest. While the children of the classes mentioned above were being initiated from the cradle into the cares of life and the prices of things, his days were spent in cloudless serenity. With no foreboding of a grimmer world beyond, he absorbed into his nature with unconscious thoroughness the beauty of the scenes in which his lot was cast. The soft beauties of the Isle of Wight, varied by the sterner lines of Northumbrian scenery, were the background to his domestic peace. He moved in a circle of which his gracious parents were the centre, among beloved sisters and cousins with whom he rode and walked and climbed and recited poetry. It was the self-confidence sprung of happiness that protected him from bullying at school where he played no games and was eccentric in appearance and habits.

SWINBURNE

We can name two others who reached the confines of the world of action equally fortified by early happiness : Shakespeare and Jane Austen. Of Shakespeare it is needless to speak ; in the case of Jane Austen we may point to the perfect temper and balance of her work through a career which continued to touch the world but lightly. With Swinburne, contact with the world produced the keenest irritation : as witness the misadventures of his London life, his untoward relations with associated men, his troubles with publishers, his club experience, even his solitary proposal of marriage. It is therefore inevitable that for the modern reader nine-tenths of his work has ceased to hold charm, and the remainder does so by virtue of that wonderful experience and heritage of joy.

If we examine the work of a contemporary we shall find something similar. There are critics who exalt Morris's *Defence of Guenevere* above all his work ; others, with more justice, his *Poems by the Way*. To the first we would remark how little of the author's inner self is expressed ; to the second, that the social reformer is present with the poet. There are still others who prefer the latter half of *The Earthly Paradise*, especially the *Lovers of Gudrun*,—or the mighty achievement of *Sigurd*. The exception we take to these is that they are not wholly informed by a living spirit. We would rather point to the unique beauty of the Greek stories of the first half of *The Earthly Paradise*. There will be found Morris's soul most fully disengaged from worldly cares and revelling in its native beauty : though we admit that the lack of a finished severity of form denies the claim of these stories, in an advanced age of literature, to the very highest poetry.

So long as man inhabits the earth he consists of soul and body, and must therefore deliver his message in earthly writing ; and thus the greatest works of imagination carry with them the seeds of their own mortality. It is the critic's duty to insist jealously upon the exclusion

of sense from the guiding intellect. The highest
Teacher bade us take no thought for the morrow, and
warned us against the materializing effect of " care " ;
and Swinburne has himself affirmed that anger is a
sensual passion. Let us listen to a song of Morris's
where the lover cannot enjoy the beautiful scenes through
which he is wending with his mistress for thought of
the great city just visible from the hill-top :

> " Hark the March wind again of a people is telling ;
> Of the life that they live there, so haggard and grim,
> That if we and our love amidst them had been dwelling,
> My fondness had faltered, thy beauty grown dim."

We see how care and anxiety and social doubts intrude
upon the amount of pure intellect needed to frame the
divine message,—so that its moral value will outlive
its æsthetic. His garden of song is surrounded by a
stone wall instead of insensibly becoming one with
the near fields and blue distances. It is not for the
intellect to be attenuated into invisibility but rather
attracted into the nature of the spirit it protects : as
the gates of iron and adamant pictured by Milton were
eternally impaled by circling fire yet unconsumed.

Thus we say a poet reveals his individual self and
becomes known to his place and age by the quality of
his spiritualized intellect. His soul in its original
essence may be one with that of the universe, but its
union with the body constitutes his life on earth,—
and we conceive of earthly life as a stage in spiritual
progress towards perfection. With Swinburne it was
contact with literature superimposed upon his inherited
and acquired experience of happiness, that directed his
pen in moments of inspiration. As he is the healthiest,
he is the least personal and most objective of poets,
the freest from morbid self-questionings, and with no
autobiographical basis to speak of in his best work.
The *Triumph of Time* is a moving poem, and there is
a special charm in his poems on children, but we do

not rate these as his best ; while his inferior work and his critical writings display that intense irritation from collision with the world of which we have spoken. It is the mystic agreement between the finished product of another mind and the vision of beauty lying in the depths of his nature—like the mysterious lake of Gaube which he delights to describe—which release his Delphic words and the waves of heavenly music on which they are borne to the listener's ear.

That Swinburne is at his best in his joyful reception and rendering of natural beauty, we maintain ; and we proceed to dwell upon the special quality which he has contributed to the work of his predecessors. When Chaucer writes,

> " Bifel that in that seson on a day
> In Southwerk at the Tabard as I lay——"

When Shakespeare sings through Ariel,

> " Come unto these yellow sands
> And then take hands——"

When Wordsworth writes of the cuckoo,

> " Though babbling only to the vale
> Of sunshine and of flowers——"

we feel that in every case the poet's great joy has trans-figured into the ideal a simple statement of fact, and made audible the music of the spheres. There is something similar in the following lines of Swinburne :

> " O gracious city well-beloved,
> Italian, and a maiden crowned,
> Siena, my feet are no more moved
> Toward thy strange-shapen mountain-bound."

But if we turn to Shakespeare's song of Marianna,

> " Take, O, take those lips away
> That so sweetly were forsworn——"

or of the bereaved Ophelia,

"White his shroud as the mountain snow
Larded with sweet flowers——"

a new note is heard from the pressure of grief upon the complex modern soul.

The complexity of the modern soul : these words are the key to the peculiar emotion rendered by Swinburne. For the modern poet does not give large circular glances at the world around but peers deeply into the inherited world within, and, like a geologist boring through the strata, discovers older civilizations and prehistoric remains. It is his duty to make articulate the human emotion which has not perished with the fleshly envelope of those who once peopled the shadowy regions, and which we may yet discover in the eyes of some haunted modern man. The cries that reach us from these submerged lands may be faint compared to our loud tones, but they are strange and beautiful, and there is a peculiar charm in the mingling of old and new, as the poet sounds the various stops. He may rise from the depth to the surface at one stroke, as when he interjects the words, " O sweet strange elder singer," amid the wild unearthly music of *Ave Atque Vale ;* or, as in *Atalanta,* his voice may take a tone from each of the strata through which it passes, and yet emerge a human voice, akin to the voices of to-day. Other writers—the Brontës, Pater, Thomas Hardy— have drawn upon this inheritance, but Swinburne differs in that the breeze which rises from the well-shaft of the soul is laden with joy rather than sorrow.

We will once more recur to the father of English poetry and the device of contrasted passages. Here are the words Chaucer puts into the mouth of the dying Arcite :

" Allas the wo ! allas the peynës stronge
That I for yow have suffred, and so long !
Allas the deeth ! allas myn Emelye !
Allas, departing of our compaignye ! . . .
What is this world ? what asketh men to have ?
Now with his love, now in his coldë grave
Allone, without any compaignye . . ."

It is the universal cry of bereaved humanity : the love of life, the fear of death and the darkness and silence of the grave, the homesickness for joys snatched away. For reality and poignancy we cannot compare the following lines from Swinburne's *Garden of Proserpine*, like murmurs from the hollow land :

> " She waits for each and other,
> She waits for all men born,
> Forgets the earth her mother,
> The life of fruits and corn."

Yet with Chaucer it is the cry of a soul bounded by walls of flesh ; with Swinburne it has the remoteness of past existences and unmeasured time.

Thus it is the undertone of Swinburne's works that concerns us, not their superficial aspect or direct intention. Surely no one's faith has ever been shaken by *Ilicet* or the *Hymn to Proserpine*,—like Tennyson's by the famous passage of Lucretius,—no one incited to vice by *Dolores*. There is regret, but of no poignant kind, in *Hesperia*, which certainly contains one of the most beautiful cadences in English poetry :

> " For thee, in the stream of the deep tide-wind blowing in with the
> water."

The true motive of the poem on the death of Baudelaire is praise for work well done, not grief for an earthly presence that has disappeared.

Perhaps the latter, and the *Prelude* to *Songs before Sunrise*, tell us the deepest secret of Swinburne's soul. We will for the moment prefer the *Ave Atque Vale* and repeat its crowning stanza :

> " Now all strange hours and all strange loves are over,
> Dreams and desires and sombre songs and sweet,
> Hast thou found place at the great knees and feet
> Of some pale Titan-woman like a lover,
> Such as thy vision here solicited,

SWINBURNE

Under the shadow of her fair vast head,
The deep division of prodigious breasts,
The solemn slope of mighty limbs asleep,
The weight of awful tresses that still keep
The savour and shade of old-world pine forests
    Where the wet hill-winds weep ? ''

With the exception of " dreams and desires " there is
no single conventional thought, no single idea that has
not been fetched from the world of echoes. It is the
perfect speech of one who, like Pater's Mona Lisa,
knows the secrets of the grave. It is the flower of his
life and culture, the spark kindled by the intellect falling
upon the soul, and thence lighting up the long downward
passages into the half-ghostly land.

It is thus that we interpret Swinburne's special
contribution to his generation,—that we re-translate
in abstract terms the divine fragments which he overheard from the angelic host who are choiring through
eternity. It is the infinite suggestion of new Americas,
full of strangeness and beauty, to be discovered in our
souls,—but with grief subtracted.

And yet the very fineness of Swinburne's gift prevents
the acceptance of the great bulk of his work, and no
poet would be a greater gainer from selection. After
constant re-reading we recur to the opinion which
recent criticism has endeavoured to disturb, that his
later poems were but an echo of his exquisite early work.
Surely a volume headed by *Atalanta*, with selections
from *Songs of the Springtides* and *Tristram of Lyonesse*,
and about a score of short poems, including those
mentioned in the foregoing pages, might descend the
stream of time with the *Lamia* volume of Keats.

If the result with Swinburne of contact with the
world was to create an irritation, in the agony of which
he forgot his early happiness and produced inferior
poetry, this is still more marked with his prose. Having
once admitted the immense value of his critical writings,
let us say that as soon as his message is accepted by the

world, and his teachings by repetition become common-places, they will inevitably disappear, for the sound reason that they give pain rather than pleasure to the reader. He is among those writers who deny equality with their readers, who lack sympathy with ordinary uninspired humanity, who assume the office of master but not master and friend. It may be spiritual pride that erects the barrier, or superior knowledge or culture, but in all cases there is something of the pedagogue. Such are Ben Jonson, Milton, Dr. Johnson, Gibbon, Macaulay, Lockhart, Herbert Spencer, Lord Morley, Mr. Arthur Symons. Of the opposite kind we may instance Scott who, it is said, treated his readers like his guests. It is distressing to accuse in this way Dr. Johnson, the friendliest of men, but it is one more proof that he was not true to himself in his writings. Having in mind a few passages in Lord Morley's *Recollections*, we are tempted to excise his name. The note of the pedagogue is not present where it might be expected, in Matthew Arnold or Jowett. It is a mere feint with Meredith, however removed his style above the mob of minds ; and it appears but fleetingly with Carlyle, for all Carlyle's philosophy is underpropped by the emotion that life is both sweet and precarious.

But Swinburne throughout his prose work handles the weapon of superior knowledge with imperfect temper and sympathy. It is admitted that except on Victor Hugo and Landor his critical verdicts have eclipsed the wisest of his predecessors and contemporaries. He was, as Ruskin said, a mighty scholar, and the perfect health and balance of his nature are almost as present in his literary judgments as in his early poetry. He encircles the whole world of ancient and modern litera-ture in his clasp,—Greek, Latin, Italian, French, English. He compares Byron and Juvenal, Webster and Sophocles, Æschylus and Shakespeare, with absolutely sure instinct and freedom from prejudice. With an almost sublime confidence in his ear to detect distinct strains of music,

he points to the scenes or even separate passages or
lines by Shakespeare, in a play of joint authorship.
The keen edge of his critical instrument is never turned
by use ; his unsleeping power of concentration enables
him to detect the one golden grain in the sandy waste
of dullness. He has not cast the essay in a form of
beauty like Arnold and Pater, but—like Darwin compared to other professors of evolution—he has gone
that one step further than the greatest which compels
them to acknowledge him the master. He rigidly
enforces the law to which all others do lip-homage :
that the artist is a specialist and must be judged by his
work only. He is therefore not deterred in his advance
to the heart of the city by the sign-posts pointing to the
moral and political and domestic quarters. No extra-
literary considerations deflect his needle by even a
tremor from its steadfast adherence to the æsthetic
north. He tells us what we knew but could not express :
that Shelley is to Coleridge as a lark to a nightingale ;
that Wordsworth's genius at its highest is sublimity in
tenderness ; that loveliness is the prime quality of
Keats ; that in rendering nature Shelley utters a
" rhapsody of thought and feeling coloured by contact
with nature but not born of the contact " ; that the gist
of Byron's philosophy is that excess brings reaction ;
that only Marlowe among poets started with a style
of his own ; that Shakespeare is a darker fatalist than
Æschylus,—and also that he cared more for literary
fame than his critics suppose. It is an anxious moment
when his eye is turned upon one of our favourites :
we sigh with relief when he appears well disposed
towards Dr. Johnson. Our fell of hair almost rises
when he advances as reason for Arnold's anti-Philistin-
ism the fact that he came of Philistine stock—David
the son of Goliath—and in the blindness of reaction
took the French Academy and *Revue des Deux Mondes*
at their own valuation. He tells us that it is the artist's
duty to suggest, not assert, and in the same breath he

applauds Balzac as " the greatest direct expounder of actual moral fact " : so assured is he that in art it is the result that weighs, independent of the process. Like the flatterers and parasites of the nobleman in Goldsmith's *Citizen of the World*, we can only tag his observations with a " Very true ! " Sorely against our will we compare to his advantage the flower of his culture springing from a rich loamy soil deposited by centuries, and Arnold's which is a comparatively new thing, and overbright with surprise and paradox.

But we must repeat that we read his essays for their matter entirely, and the author is never our friend : though always with the reminder that the cause is the action of the world on a nature incomparably fine. He overpowers us with his superior knowledge, and frightens us with the impatience and irascibility of the pedagogue. When Professor Bradley in his book on Shakespeare quotes Swinburne, we feel a relief that it is Bradley not Swinburne with whom we are walking. The law that taste is no matter for dispute is suspended in his favour ; we suppress in our minds any admiration for Euripides or Musset or the *Idylls of the King*, much as a schoolboy hides a detective story under a grammar or dictionary ; or we recall our readings of the *Duchess of Malfi* and doubt whether we admired heartily enough to escape the modern Dunciad. At moments, indeed, through the parted clouds of anger we see the blue skies of poetry,—as when he compares *Childe Harold* and *Don Juan* to lake water and sea water, or the effect of Chapman's translation of Homer to the pace of a giant for echo of the footfall of a God ;—and a bright-bannered host marches down his processional road through the land of Shakespeare. But for the most part he is in a state of warfare against real or imaginary fools. Dr. Johnson, writing of Milbourne's attack on Dryden's *Virgil*, would have revised his opinion that bad poetry alone cannot excite strong resentment, had he known how completely Swinburne lived in and for literature.

And here, after having given almost involuntarily the highest tribute to the man of letters, we ask the final question : how far was this life complete ? It is the more pertinent with Swinburne because he professed the belief that earthly life suffices for man. He extolled Frederick the Great because he fought " sober " and was not " God-intoxicated " like the Puritans, and affirmed that heroism was spoilt for him by trust in Providence. That he was spiritually-minded we know from his fervid hero-worship and reiterated confession that his acquaintance with Landor and Mazzini, even his correspondence with Hugo, had been the greatest privileges of his life. Of the first event he wrote, " I am not sure that any other emotion is so endurable and persistently delicious as that of worship, when your god is indubitable and incarnate before your eyes." With this we may compare the following : " I don't myself know any pleasure physical or spiritual (except what comes of the sea) comparable to that which comes of verse in its higher moods."

It is a fascinating theory, in an agnostic age, that human life and the full development of the faculties suffice man's highest needs, and that death may thus lose its sting. Here at least is no promise of a remote inheritance that may founder with all our hopes, but something that we possess this day. Yet we recall Newman's picture of the heathen writers yearning in vain for some unknown good and higher truth, and the words of Lucretius which he quotes : " We should be happy were it not for that dreadful sense of Religion which we all have, which poisons all our pleasures——" Also we have in our minds Carlyle's unforgettable pictures of the great actors of the eighteenth century who have passed the peak of years and are treading the slope towards the tomb,—and the deathbeds of kings or statesmen or voluptuaries who believed in the reality of power or pleasure. Though comparisons are not always fair, as we turn the pages of a man's life we unconsciously try it by an ideal, and the ideal life (shall we say ?) is St. Paul's, to whom, as years passed on, the unseen world became more vivid and the material world more faint.

In Shakespeare's day the balance between inner and outer was equally maintained : on Milton and the Puritan reaction we need not dwell. The eighteenth century saw the dawn of the belief in the reality of human life, which, in the nineteenth, was to culminate in the pursuit of material efficiency and the real-policy of commerce. How the poets were affected by the prevailing spirit we see from the ages of Dryden, Addison, Pope, Johnson, when the muse had left her solitudes to frequent the tavern or coffee house. But even before the French Revolution the reaction had set in, and the tragedies of Burns and Byron illustrate the revolt from the social world of those who were dependent on its sympathies and enslaved by its memories.

Perhaps Swinburne above all poets—above even Tennyson who stopped at the half-way house of fame— was true to himself. If human life alone can satisfy the soul, he enjoyed to the full three of its most splendid gifts : hero-worship, friends, fame : and if a poet values fame for the sake of love and admiration rather than power, his measure was indeed filled to overflowing. It was his custom to recite his unpublished poems to friends, and we can imagine few greater transports of the soul than to intone as new things to a sympathetic audience the long lines of *Hesperia* or the *Hymn to Proserpine*. What the rude external world did was to break the silver cord of poetic inspiration and darken with anger his critical writings, yet he held an unbroken course. In the beautiful conclusion of Sir Edmund Gosse's biography we see him become the shadow of his former self, brooding over dead friends and the " wonderful days of his youth." Recalling what was said of comparative lives, and preferring to conceive of the world as a place of hope, it saddens us to hear that in his latest years he wrote verses " to escape from boredom." But he was strong-nerved as well as fine-nerved, and was never persuaded to recant or decline from his position that this life is all, or profess the star-lit faiths of some agnostics weakened by bereavement or old age. His gifts were lyric genius and health of race and person, and the tinge of the second is in his immortal work : it is in the brightness of the ray of this world's sunshine which he darted into the pale kingdoms inherited by the soul.

The Homeland of Jane Austen

THE HOME-LAND OF JANE AUSTEN

THE children who set out to chase the rainbow may still, in old age, be toiling across country towards that brilliant phenomenon, but the mere observer has learnt on what day of rain and sun to look from his window. Even so the critic, baffled by the Nile-sources of genius, is free to speculate on the influence on genius of the circumstances of its owner's life. And with Jane Austen it was her happiness which quickened her insight and gave her power to draw character with a balance only attained by the greatest. She was absolutely happy in her home circle, and in performing the small duties of life and enjoying its daily pleasures. She lived far from the literary world, and though she did care for fame as an author, was but slightly troubled at the long delay between the writing of her early novels and their publication. Genius is said to be eccentric and self-conscious, but not only was she neither, but to the end of her days she thought that her sister's powers of mind surpassed her own.

That she was absorbed by home doings and scarcely heeded public events, strikes us more when we reflect on the vast changes that occurred within her lifetime. She was born in 1775 and died in 1817, and within those forty-two years occurred the French Revolution and the wars of Napoleon. Not only was every institution shaken to its base, and every country on the continent of Europe overrun, but a profound change took place in the soul of man. How the external events affected her may be judged from the following passages in her letters. At the beginning of the Peninsular War she writes : " I am sorry to find that Sir John Moore has a mother living, but though a very heroic son he might not be a very necessary one to her happiness." And again : " How horrible it is to have so many people killed ! And what a blessing that one cares for none of them ! " The inner changes failed equally to perturb her eighteenth-century manner of thinking. At the present day such a person would be called narrow-minded or self-absorbed, but let no one bring a charge of this kind against Jane Austen.

We know on the great authority of the late W. P. Ker that the eighteenth century was not the age of prose it has been thought. Writers who stayed at home or consorted with a few friends through their lives, were no strangers to the divine idea of the universe. The lightning of the French Revolution struck the peasant's cottage as well as the king's palace, and thereafter fear was born into the world. The barbarians who destroyed the Roman Empire came from the far north, but the modern highly organized State breeds her own destroy-ers,—in mine and factory and workshop, in overcrowded slum and tenement and tangled network of mean streets. To stay at home, to meditate, to enjoy the small pleasures of life, has become impossible ; and where fear is no spiritual progress can be. Therefore the poet strains violently to salve the deep-sunken romance in his nature by illicit love-making or exploiting nature's terrific moods. Like Scott he may turn to the legends of the past ; like Byron or Châteaubriand, wander over the globe and stimulate his sense of wonder with inaccessible mountains or primeval forests. He cannot enjoy the present unless he forgets himself, and the divine idea is hidden from those who do not enjoy the present : but the men and women of the eighteenth century needed not to forget themselves to enjoy the present.

Certain philosophers affirm that every natural object

contains the divine idea, which is the only reality, and is revealed to the contemplating mind. The ordinary person is no philosopher, but the power to love may replace the power to contemplate. We revisit the scenes of the happy past, where we walked with our friends, and recover the old emotion as forgotten details strike the eye,—the gate between two fields, the winding of the road, the sun setting behind the clump of trees, and the afterglow burning in the clear sky above their tops : but the country that surrounds the home of an unhappy past is a dead thing. The happiness first arising in the heart spreads to surrounding things : as the poem learned by the child and repeated by the aged man recalls the child's home and earliest friends and all the details of his life. We seek happiness, therefore, from no selfish motive, but to find our souls and realize the world is divine. Happiness on earth is one of the inner proofs of immortality.

Jane Austen's happiness stayed rather at the centre of things—the human heart. She does not seem to have attached herself strongly to the scenes in which her life was set. There are gaps in her letters, but those we have at the time of the break-up of her early home at Steventon, where she spent the first twenty-five years of her life, reveal no poignant sorrow. It sufficed that the home circle was unbroken : and indeed, while she lived, she lost no one of her dearest except her father. She and her sister Cassandra were once described in a letter as " elegant young women," and they were lively and good-looking, and certainly attracted men, yet fate willed they should not marry. The clergyman to whom Cassandra was betrothed died of yellow fever in the West Indies, and Jane's one suitor who is thought to have deserved her, died soon after the acquaintance opened. Another who possessed " all but the subtle power of touching her heart," did propose and was accepted ; but her mind immediately changed, and she preferred to keep the joys she had rather than fly to others that she knew not of. Her age was twenty-seven, and she and her sister were visiting old friends in Hampshire. Their hosts drove them back to their brother's house and took tearful and distressing farewells : after which they required their brother to accompany them by coach to their home at Bath, though he could ill spare the time. This action, so contrary to their usual considerate selves, shows how Jane's balance of mind was overthrown by the danger to old associations.

The author of the *Memoir* remarks that there were no disagreements in the Austen family, and they never disputed or argued. He thus pays a tribute to delicacy and self-control under the hard conditions where daily passages increase the risk to be familiar. To speak one's mind on every occasion shows rather a lacking sense of decency than a love of truth : and that the faculties are stimulated by contradiction is one of those half-truths which the world has agreed to pass round like paper money. A letter is extant written by the father to his son Francis—after to become Admiral—then in his fifteenth year, and about to embark as a volunteer on a frigate for the East Indies. The letter is described as wise and kind, and remarkable for the courtesy and delicacy with which the father advises his son, who was but a boy, but whom he treats as an officer. Another typical thing is Jane's conduct to her beloved niece Fanny, whose love-confidences she received, but spoke of them to no third person, not even to the sister from whom she was inseparable. We may also recall how, in her last years of illness, Jane improvised a sofa with chairs lest her mother should use less frequently the only sofa in their home. Domestic happiness is therefore a separate art, and by no means one easy to practise ; and now if we look back to the words about Sir John Moore we understand that a man's loss is not deeper felt because he wins battles and conducts retreats. Indeed those of us who have absorbed King Lear's terrible sayings about the official world, may think less of the great ones of the earth ; but while honouring the Austen family as ideal, it is not here intended to praise indiscriminately all self-sufficing families, for there is a narrow and exclusive domestic affection, nourished on suspicion of those outside, which is by no means pleasing to look upon : and yet Froude said truly that disguise is impossible within the home circle—that he who is loved by brother or sister cannot be bad.

Granted the sound family traditions and the self-control and other good qualities of individual members, it remains to see the effect of this happiness on Jane Austen's work. To her assured position she owed her perfect temper and absence of concern for mere literary fame, in which she resembled Scott and Shakespeare. Her first three books, written before she was twenty-three, were not published for thirteen years, yet she did not fret over the delay. Looking at the work itself we discern a radical difference between her and all but one of the greater English novelists. The novelist who delineates a character places it in one scale and himself in another. With Dickens the caricaturist depresses the author's scale, with Thackeray the satirist, with George Eliot the philosopher, with Charlotte Brontë the lyric poet. Only with Scott and Jane Austen is there the perfect balance of Shakespeare. Each of the others desires to remould the world according to a pre-conceived plan.

That she had her philosophy as much as Thackeray, we will not dispute, and the characters of both move in groups. All Thackeray's persons play their parts within the town of Vanity, while she retains hers within the home circle ; yet there is something of the larger family life in Thackeray's conception, and he deals with the stings which those in close relation inflict upon each other. But when he actually touches the inmost circle we see how essentially they differ. It may be true or false that Amelia was an insipid character,—yet some persons hold that she is redeemed by her quarrels with her mother at the end of *Vanity Fair*. But does not the episode of the shawl which she sells to buy books for her boy make us wince with pain while we read it ? We feel a guilty pang as if we had been eavesdropping and heard what we should not. Place beside it the silver knife in *Mansfield Park* which had belonged to the dead child and proved a source of discord between two of the living. By many previous intimate touches Jane Austen has made us one of the family circle, and we realize this to be but a single phase of ill-feeling. The acutely sensitive Thackeray, unhappy in his eaaly manhood, had been cut to the quick by the world's sharp ways, and his art is less whole and perfect.

There survived into the eighteenth century, it is said, something of the sociable quality of the Middle Ages, when artists worked like members of a guild. Pope has been tried for his poetic life and acquitted after a long and memorable trial like Warren Hastings. He wrote for an audience that he knew, and by saying that Jane Austen makes us one of the family circle, we imply that hers was a social art. Her domestic affections were strongest, but not exclusive, and she was friendly with neighbours, though not intimate. She enjoyed dances and visits to London and theatres and tea-parties, and the whole social round in moderation. At the age of thirty-three she wrote : " It was the same room in which we danced fifteen years ago. I thought it all over, and in spite of the shame of being so much older, felt with thankfulness that I was quite as happy now as then." She was keenly interested in all the people she met, but rated them correctly in proportion to the distance of their circles from her inmost circle. She discriminated even nearer home, writing thus to Cassandra about their niece Fanny who was growing up : " I found her in the summer just what you describe, almost another sister ; and could not have supposed that a niece would ever have been so much to me." This social quality of Jane Austen's life is transferred to her books, and the reader becomes definitely related to her. He savours the best family gossip.

It has been said that all Thackeray's books might be called *Vanity Fair*, and we constantly feel that Becky Sharp and Arthur Pendennis and Clive Newcome are passing shadows. They reflect the mind of one who believes that all is vanity, and whose soul is therefore alone with the universe. The game of life interests him because it enables him to forget himself, but the delight is in the struggle, not in the result. For Becky who had been used as a child to cajole the unpaid milkman, it was a grand transformation scene to enter ducal halls,— but she was bored in the end. Thackeray belonged to that later generation which had inherited fear and needed strong emotions to make the world live. Macbeth cannot enjoy the crown because, in killing Duncan, he has killed his own soul, and he thinks but of the future :

> " For Banquo's issue have I filed my mind ;
> For them the gracious Duncan have I murdered ;
> Put rancours in the vessel of my peace
> Only for them, and mine eternal jewel
> Given to the common enemy of man——"

And when he hears that Lady Macbeth is dead :

> " She should have died hereafter ;
> There would have been a time for such a word."

To him as to all those who cannot enjoy the present, the world has become a dead place, and he already tastes annihilation.

FitzGerald, Thackeray's contemporary, described as one of his impressions from Boswell's *Life of Johnson*, that all the persons who acted so busily were now gone. Jane Austen's characters act busily enough ; they taste the small pleasures of life ; they desire to get married and live in comfortable houses : and we never think that time is passing and all must end. At first sight she seems to lack the idealizing touch of the later

" romantics." In Mrs. Gaskell's little town of Cranford, for instance, it is always afternoon : the characters are sheltered from the rough winds of life, and their charm is increased by their narrow means and shifts to live respectably. Jane Austen is under no illusions as to the power of money, and we almost smile when again and again she mentions the exact figure of her heroines' dowries. But this is no surrender to the charge of prose which the eighteenth century now disclaims. It asserts, against the fevered, galvanized social doings of Thackeray,—and the mountain-climbing, desert-travers-ing " romantics "—the joys of home, where, untroubled by economics, the soul develops the power to enjoy the present which is immortal life.

Of this happiness we would like further details, but the letters give few intimate revelations, and the published biographical matter is slight. Now and then the letters afford a picture—such as this written from Godmersham in 1813 : " The comfort of the billiard-table here is very great : it draws all the gentlemen to it whenever they are within, especially after dinner, so that my brother, Fanny, and I have the library to ourselves in delightful quiet." And again : " Billiards again drew all the odd ones away, and Edward, Charles, the two Fannies and I sat snugly talking." It was this summer which saw the friendship with her niece Fanny develop, and she speaks of their " delicious mornings." About the same time she wrote to her brother Frank on the subject of authorship : " After all, what a trifle it is, in all its bearings, to the really important points of one's exist-ence, even in this world." She published her novels anonymously, and it was against her will that her name finally became known. She even avoided literary circles, once declining to meet Madame de Staël at a party of wits. She lived content among intellectual inferiors, and differed notably from later-born writers, who not only sought out tremendous scenes in nature but craved to know distinguished persons—requiring the full blast of a great human presence to make them believe man has a soul,—instead of waiting patiently to be convinced of it by the small daily events among those who are humble-minded, but also unselfish, self-controlled, and earthly-refined. The criticism that Jane Austen excelled because she wrote of what she knew is fair,—but what she knew was divine.

If we leave her life and examine her art we find in it the same philosophy. The test she applies to her characters is whether or not they are good members of the republic of home. The perfect balance that made us compare her with Scott and Shakespeare is not thereby disturbed, for she does not obtrude her philosophy like Thackeray or Balzac, or utter Charlotte Brontë's lyric cry. But since her own position was well assured, she asked nothing of the larger world, and if she lacked partners at a dance, or publishers declined her first novels, she had too many compensations nearer home to be hurt. Therefore she had the impartial touch of the two great ones mentioned above, whose first ambitions were not literary, and who were above literary jealousies. But she was none the less keenly interested in the world's doings, and no doubt delighted to talk over her social adventures with members of her family,—and here we have the spirit of her writings. They contain the essence of the finest gossip : that is the confidential talk of open-minded friends over the foibles or virtues of a larger circle,—and, since the art is a social one, there is an inevitable point of view,—an inevitable, if unconscious, comparison of the minds and circumstances of the speakers with those spoken of.

It may sound impertinent to affirm that anything written by Jane Austen is crude, but all terms are relative, and this one is used here by contrast with the surpassingly fine work which she afterwards achieved. In *Sense and Sensibility* we are conscious of three interests, imperfectly related artistically, though finally reconciled by the author's personality. There are the major characters, the minor characters, and the story. It is her earliest book and the one we could best spare and are most inclined to omit in re-reading her works ; for, excepting Marianne's absorbing and elemental passion for Willoughby—a theme that does not distinguish Jane Austen among novelists—there is little that we do not find better done later. Lady Middleton whose calmness of manner was reserve rather than sense, suggests Lady Bertram ; Lucy Steele who does not see that her confidences are unwelcome, suggests Mrs. Elton ; and Mr. Palmer who is deliberately rude to his mother-in-law, and draws his wife's comment, " Mr. Palmer is so droll ! he is always out of humour," is a first draft of the finely discriminated John Knightley household. They are preliminary studies, as the wit-combats of Biron and Rosaline foreshadow those of Benedick and Beatrice, and the mistaken identities of the *Comedy of Errors* those of *Twelfth Night*. The author asserts—she is not to be blamed for this, for her art is a social one and pre-supposes a court of appeal—but here she over-asserts. As she turns from each figure the light goes out, and the next with whom she busies herself is untouched by the former beam. Or the figures are disposed in a half-circle, and must step backwards to seek each other, instead of intermingling by moving easily round in a complete circle. They instance her views on life—the true or false domestic or social or domestic-social virtue, and how far foiled or stimulated by education, position, nature. Of course this applies to the minor characters, and even there Lucy Steele tends to emerge and become an individual. As revealing the author's dawning method the book interests, but in view of the treasures that await us it interests little for its own sake, and we can leave it half studied.

Jane Austen never changed her philosophy but she advanced in the art which expressed it. In *Pride and Prejudice* she has taken all but her last step in art, though we are not among those who place it first of her works. In the earlier book, for the first and last time, appeared a conventional strain, learned from other novels,— such as the duel between Willoughby and Brandon ; but here she begins to draw on nothing but her own experience. The outer art of *Pride and Prejudice* is perfect, and if we discover a fault it is by contrast with a more fully united later art, where hand and heart and experience moved together. The fault is a certain deliberate exaggeration of the follies of the small world she depicted, as if to make them better material for gossip. We feel that the absurdities of Mrs. Bennet and Mr. Collins are being noted so as to be retailed to congenial friends amid peals of laughter. For pure humour it would be hard to match the scene where Mr. Collins introduces himself to Darcy, and the anxious Elizabeth, from the movement of his lips, detects the word " apology." But when Mary sings before the guests with her weak voice and affected manner, and Elizabeth perceives the two younger sisters making signs of derision at each other,—and when at the end of the evening she concludes that her family could hardly have exposed themselves more had they tried to do so,— we are approaching the dangerous ground of Thackeray, where we are not members of the family but eaves-droppers. Jane Austen never faltered in her belief that a person's character is best tried by family life, that good manners and principles can be assumed in outer circles,—and with greater success the more remote ; but at this early stage she dwelt rather on the outer circle of family life where it touches intimate social life. And as the chief business of this latter life is marriage, much must be conceded to appearances and the good opinion of the world. Hence Mrs. Bennet is condemned less for trying her daughters' tempers at home than creating prejudice with desirable suitors. Jane Austen is never bitter, but she depicts Mr. and Mrs. Bennet, and their younger daughters, and Mr. Collins, and Bingley's sisters, with a humour that is salted. Mr. Bennet had married a woman whom he could not now respect, and he compensated himself by making her look ridiculous before her children, and enjoying the situation when his family exposed itself in public. In reality this is not a thing to laugh at, but it becomes so through the author's youth and high spirits. It is the point of view of one who does not suffer from the evil she depicts, but observes it in order to extract humour from it among her assured friends and equals. She had not learnt that her own life was exceptional, and that perfect domestic happiness is an art not to be achieved by the many.

The two books just discussed, though first written, were carefully revised in later years, so perhaps *Northanger Abbey* is the fairest entire specimen of her early work. While the novice still shows in plot and construction, there begins that delicate inwardness which made the fortune of the later books, though, compared to *Persuasion*, it is like water-colour beside miniature painting. The plot may be said to fail partially at the point where it joins the characters ; the satire on Mrs. Radcliffe's novels being forcibly imposed upon the heroine's temperament. Jane Austen is still over-conscious that she is writing a novel and must fit her experience into a form accepted by the popular mind. Contrasts of character are emphasised too strongly, such as Catherine with Isabella Thorpe, and Tilney with John Thorpe. Of the minor characters, Mrs. Allen who did not talk much but could never be entirely silent, and observed everything aloud, advances greatly on those of *Sense and Sensibility*, though compared to Lady Bertram she is like a cut flower to one rooted in the soil of the story.

But it is Catherine Morland who truly concerns us, and the interest is with her change of mood. Her happiness waxes and wanes, and the effect is like a landscape which glows in the sunlight or darkens under cloud. She was humble-minded, as her creator is said to have been, but she had an unfailing test for character : its effect on her unspoilt, receptive mind. She believed John Thorpe was a fine fellow, because he told her so ; she believed his great doings with his College friends, and that he was an accomplished whip—though his horse, when " let go," did not prance and rear as he had foretold. Yet after an hour or so of his company she felt a weariness that she could not explain. And when she is with her dear friends, the Tilneys, she is shocked to find how much her spirits are relieved when their father withdraws. It is her changes of mood that create the entire atmosphere at Northanger Abbey—her scruple that she has stayed too long—her delight in being reassured and earnestly pressed to stay. On the last sorrowful morning, at breakfast, she contrasts the happiness of twenty-four hours ago when Henry sat beside her, and also the first miles of journey along the road she had travelled ten days since. Where she reflects her creator is in the power to extract happiness from these small day to day events. The interest of the book is inward but not subjective in the modern sense,—for the movements of Catherine's mind depend upon those of other minds. She is still like a child who cannot understand the true nature of sorrow, but feels it in the hushed laughter and downcast looks of her usual grown-up playmates. It is here that we see the gulf between Jane Austen and the " romantics " : for the romantic soul grows in solitude, and uses social life merely to express its strange experience. But if this book is imperfect it is because so delicate a mind requires less strong contrasts than the suggestions of Mrs. Radcliffe, the rough manners and want of sensitiveness of the Thorpes, and the rudeness of General Tilney ;—but the perfectly graded work was to be duly achieved.

Northanger Abbey was completed in 1798, and for nearly thirteen years after Jane Austen was silent. The early spring of 1801 saw the break-up of her home at Steventon, and removal to Bath, where in February, 1805, her father died. Next year the family left Bath for Southampton, and in 1809 settled at Chawton where Jane spent the last eight years of her life. There she finally revised and published her first two novels, and in February, 1811, at the age of thirty-five, began *Mansfield Park*. Art is not a matter for amateurs and requires constant practice,—but it also requires long inactive periods ; and we shall now see how fruitfully the unconscious mind had worked.

In *Mansfield Park* she is working upon the interior lines where plot cannot be separated from character. The characters are presented in contrasts, and as the daily happenings of family life in a country house develop the characters and therefore the contrasts, the plot moves. Imperceptibly it gathers force, which at the end is suddenly released, and we get Maria's elopement and Julia's runaway marriage ; and the light flashed upon the reader strikes back through the breadth of the book and the characters grouped in his imagination. Jane Austen is as happy as ever, but experience has taught her to laugh less lightly at mere outer peculiarities. Her balance is surer because she does not deliberately search for matter to laugh at, and her temper even more perfect. We are now in the heart of her country or home-land where characters are tested by their power to please within the family circle. Lady Bertram, who thinks nothing can be dangerous or fatiguing to anyone but herself, succumbs to this test ; so does Sir Thomas who wishes to be kind but is too grave in manner ; and so does their eldest son who consoles himself for the consequences of extravagance by the thought that he is less in debt than his friends. Critics have called Edmund a prig and been bored by Fanny Price, but they forget that the standards of the family are not those of the world.

Fanny is like a highly sensitized instrument that registers the smallest disturbance in the family calm.

When Sir Thomas leaves for Antigua, and his daughters are indifferent, she alone grieves because she cannot grieve. She also misses and regrets her cousins, though they have never been actively kind to her. The defect of the strong and external contrasts of *Northanger Abbey* is remedied beyond all doubt. Against her will Mary Crawford prefers Edmund, though he is neither man of the world nor elder brother. Henry Crawford is drawn imperceptibly into Fanny's orbit, away from the brilliant cousins. Maria had felt Crawford's lively personality, and dreads her approaching marriage to the rich but commonplace Rushworth. Their education has tainted their minds, and their manners and persons are better than their hearts, but none the less they have hearts that can recognise goodness. It is true that Mrs. Norris is shown without a redeeming feature, except that she would manage better in the place of her poorer sister—Fanny's mother : but the situation is saved by humour. Like Mrs. Bennet and Mr. Collins she provides laughter for the gossips : as when in the final ruins of the abandoned theatricals she appropriates the green baize curtain. We also complained in *Northanger Abbey* that a character like Mrs. Allen, however amusing, merely played on the surface of the story. Compare her sayings with that of Lady Bertram when the theatricals are first bruited : " Do not act anything improper, my dear, Sir Thomas would not like it." How much it tells us why the moral world of Mansfield Park is out of joint ! Yet Fanny regrets her adopted home when she revisits her own family, and of all contrasts this is the most skilful. Life must be economically based, and Mansfield Park was at least externally well ordered, while in her own home her father swore and called out for rum and water, her mother rated the servants, her sisters quarrelled, the food was coarse and badly served, the meals unpunctual, the noise incessant——. But through this, as through the faults or weaknesses of all its characters, we discern why *Mansfield Park* leaves a total impression that satisfies. The imperfect world is so presented that it suggests an ideal world of calm happiness, not too remote to be attained, and which is attained by two of the chief actors in the comedy.

Fanny grows upon us till her spirit informs the whole. As the others are tried and found wanting, she quietly assumes their virtues—for they are not without them—and becomes strong enough to bear the weight of the plot alone. Lady Bertram cannot do without her ; Sir Thomas multiplies attentions, culminating in a dance in her honour ; Henry Crawford has forgotten Maria and Julia and desires only her ; and Edmund at last prefers her to Mary Crawford,—though the latter concealed a good heart under a worldly crust, and looked lovely when she smiled. Coriolanus addressed his wife as " My gracious silence,"—and the most spiritual people prevail by silence. Not only do the virtues of the others pass into her, but even their good looks. " Fanny looked so lovely," said Crawford to explain his lengthened visit at Mansfield. We recall the words of Pandarus about Cressida to the love-sick Troilus : " Well, she looked yesternight fairer than ever I saw her look, or any woman else——" And among the company of women was Helen of Troy !

Emma is a work of perfect art, but loses by the chronological reading of Jane Austen. In *Mansfield Park* we were in the deeps of her mind ; here we retire one step outward into the region of mixed family and social life. It is that of *Pride and Prejudice,* but mellowed and ripened, with a richer humour, higher technical skill, and nearer to imaginative truth. In the earlier book it was possible that a love-story like that of Elizabeth and Darcy might have so developed and run its course, but between it and the inner relations of their natures was an undoubted space. In *Emma* as in *Mansfield Park* plot and character are self-moved, though *Emma* has little plot to speak of. In *Mansfield Park* the characters had to struggle to win happiness, but here it is assured them. The outer events are weddings, dances, garden-parties, excursions, but when the last page is reached the characters are practically unchanged. Emma has learnt some lessons and gained her heart's wish by marrying Knightley and remaining with her father, but not in this lies the charm. It is rather in the contrasts of character which the social gatherings admit of, that have no active issue, yet are organic : in which the book differs markedly from *Sense and Sensibility* and shows how immeasurably Jane Austen improved her later art. We admit to preferring the middle regions of the story to its heights and depths. Emma's quarrel with Knightley about Harriet Smith and their cordial hand-shaking when they next meet, impress more than the unconscious rivalry and misunderstanding with Jane Fairfax. Not that the more heroic actions—if we may so strain the word—are superfluous, for they kindle in us a moment's doubt or fear, and therefore make us realize more truly the little world of Emma and her invalid father, and gentle Mrs. Weston whom the said father continues to pity for her marriage, despite its happiness,—and Knightley, and a few others of the inner circle. That the self-confident and insensitive Mrs. Elton should patronize Emma and inform her that " Knightley is quite the·gentleman " indeed makes us hold our breath with dismay. Yet the fear is but momentary, for the little world lies too sheltered in its hollow to be harmed from without. External events import only so far as they affect the soul in its contemplating moments when self is present to self. We pray that the relative catastrophes may be averted, the marriages take place, that our friends who marry may continue to live near us,—so that when the day's social work is done, the soul may have no regrets to mar its steady day-to-day contentment. We see this reflected in poor Miss Bates who speaks quite candidly of the sharp words Emma had addressed to her ; and in Harriet Smith whom Emma convinces again and again that she must forget Mr. Elton, without producing any effect. In the beginning Emma did not intend to marry and leave her father, yet liked to hear her name coupled with Frank Churchill's. Even so were her numerous mental misadventures in her attempts to form Harriet Smith's character and make her social fortune. The dividing line between the family and the world is inner not outer, and at times those who cross the threshold are not all-sympathetic. Emma knows what it is to be apprehensive lest her brother-in-law, John Knightley, should be impatient with her father ; and she has to invite the Eltons ; and it was not well planned to combine the two parties at Box Hill. As in southern climates where the clear air makes a small sound be heard from far off, so we feel the slightest twinge in these minds at peace with themselves : and therefore at the heart of the book there is a silence—— If Jane Austen may be approached in the Elysian fields, will she tell us why Emma was a little uncharitable to Miss Bates ?

With *Persuasion* we return to the deeper world of *Mansfield Park* and find ourselves in the very inmost circle of the writer's heart. In *Mansfield Park* the actors had to win their happiness ; in *Emma* it was assured them, but they must guard it from contagious breaths of the outer world—graded from the uneasiness of mistaken good intentions to the shock of unsympathetic intruders. *Persuasion* tells of a happiness that has been lost but is won again, and so has a double value. When Jane Austen composed it the fatal illness had already touched her, and the line of cleavage shows between the two worlds. We have stressed the practical side of her nature : that she does not treat of dowerless heroines, and realizes that a small house and narrow means and domestic worries may spoil the temper ; but here she shows us that the world can be a still harder place, that one must help oneself also, that delicacies of mind may serve their possessor ill without certain commonplace virtues such as firmness. But having touched on this she restores the balance and shows us again the two worlds made one—the ideal realized on earth. Anne Elliot in early youth had weakly let herself be persuaded to break off her engagement with Captain Wentworth. Eight years later they meet, and he is estranged, and in quest of a bride. Louisa Musgrove is pretty, lively, good-humoured, unaffected, but she lacks Anne's finer nature ; and, unwillingly at first, but with ever-accelerating pace, his spirit moves back to Anne. It is Anne's last throw for happiness, for her first youth is over, and her father and sister, wrapped in their worldly concerns, are like strangers to her. Here we see the book's higher seriousness, for if she fails she is lost : but she does not fail, and this happiness, once lost, twice gained, reveals to us an unsteadier outer world but an inner world made perfect. Because it was nearly lost it seems more precious, and because it is regained the message of the book is one of hope, though our earth is dissolving like a pageant. The walls that guard the home have thinned, and even the healthy Louisa recovers slowly from her fall on the Cobb, and the shock to her nerves is lasting.

But the world of *Persuasion* is not entirely one of sunset, and most of the characters are interested above all in life. The humour is unabated, as witness Mrs. Musgrove who, when the hard lot of naval officers and their wives is discussed, says she knows what separation is because her husband attends the assizes. But Jane Austen who so far had dealt only with life, now tells us of the sleep that rounds it ; and the cause of this added beauty was a mind preserving its power in bodily decline, yet touched by the shadow. The attempt to identify the personality of such a truly objective writer with one of her characters is dangerous, but, as in looking-glass land, the critic who disclaims it detects himself in it again and again. Jane Austen tends to develop Anne Elliot beyond the needs of the story, pointing out her favourite books and best-loved scenes in nature, such as the hues of autumn. She was sensitive to suggestion, having been persuaded to renounce her engagement, and yet over-anxious to express certain cherished thoughts. These weaknesses of the artistic nature may have appeared in her creator's latest year, though concealed throughout a healthful life. We know that she confided to her family details about her characters in their life beyond her pages. She told them that Mary Bennet married humbly, and that Mrs. Norris's gift to Fanny's brother was one pound sterling ! May we follow from a distance and add that Anne, in her own home, like her creator, preserved the strong affections and fine courtesies of domestic life—while it lasted ! Helen Faucit in her charming book on Shakespeare's heroines conjectured that Imogen did not live long after she was reunited to Posthumus : we may say the same of Anne,—and that her husband did not re-marry. He would have fared like Jane Austen's nephews and nieces who visited Chawton after her death and expected to be happy, but found the charm had disappeared.

While the novels are collected in our memory we will make a late attempt to define concisely the cause of their lasting power to please. The small doings of a small society written down with perfect balance and no prejudice, and rightly related to the whole of contemporary life, would suffice for an age rather than all time : although there are moments when an unconscious touch so transfigures these small doings that the century-clock is put back, and for a space we live in that world, among those people, on that afternoon : for instance, when Fanny looks out from a window at Mansfield and sees the two ladies—Mrs. Grant and Miss Crawford—walking up from the Vicarage. But there is also something that transcends,—partially expressed and half understood with the first, but steadily growing conscious and permeating the last. It is that every character, grave or gay, is concerned with the same thing,—either ignoring it, or mistaking it, or preventing others from attaining it, or following it by false roads, or at last truly seeking it : and that is the foretaste of immortal joy on earth. To secure it you must face facts and so manage your worldly business that you live the life of the spirit—the spirit that knows nothing of death.

Plutarch Revisited

PLUTARCH REVISITED

IF a classic is a book that is eternally fresh and can teach the last generations, there are few above Plutarch's biographies. Because present conditions have made hero-worship the dominant religion, the pagan world looks nearer across the gulf of the Middle Ages. Our world, like the Greek and Roman, absorbs all our energy, and excludes time for spiritual communion. But as man cannot do without religion, he will at least not disregard that which is thrust upon him, and is forced to worship a greater soul than his own. It is only partially true that our age is democratic, for the decline of artificial distinctions brings it home that nature has made men unequal. This is not to preach the obvious doctrine of merit ; for the complete man is no creature of a generation ; the throne is badly filled by the winner in mere competition ; and even genius cannot transfigure plebeian features. In our search for the truly great man, we must steer a middle course between the Pharisaic regard for appearances and externals of the Victorian age and the materialistic doctrines of modern democracy. We must also eliminate the highest form to which man has attained—the artist or mystic, for whom the time is not ripe,—and the lowest —the real-politician, who reminds the human race of its animal origin.

There are certain shadowed periods in the history of the world when the heavenly stars by which the human race has been used to steer are blotted out. Such was the third century of the Christian era, such is our own, when the nations of Europe exhausted by war are faced with a sterner struggle to live ; when man, as Carlyle once said, walks by the light of conflagrations and to the sound of falling cities. Insecurity begets fear, whether in the over-taxed professional man,—or the operative whom an uncertain foreign market may deprive of his work on the morrow,—or the broken-nerved leisure classes who anticipate industrial strife, and feel like a stab every look of the displaced worker, and shrink from the bitter words of the labour leaders. If we are to be saved, it can only be by our fellow-man with the stronger soul, and we have travelled far from the Victorian snobbishness depicted by Thackeray and need something more than a hereditary duke.

It sufficed the Victorians to lead an outwardly decent life, untroubled by the fear that a sudden catastrophe might end their world. The son followed in his father's steps, and few strove to exceed the sphere in which they were born. If a writer pleased once he was assured of future readers by merely imitating himself ; while now, if each successive book does not contain some new spiritual thing, he is pushed aside. In art and in human intercourse man demands reality : he has no time to play at living in a dangerous world : like the Victorians, who went to church, and dined and visited formally, and spared years to mourn for departed friends.

He is spiritual enough to crave for God, but material enough to recognize only as much of the glory of God as transfigures an earthly presence. The mind and emotions of the poet bring us nearest to heaven, but we can only accept him as Friend, not Master, for he is not at home on earth,—and it needs slight effort to recall the weaknesses and follies of men of artistic genius. But we reject entirely the man of business or real-politician, in whom is no trace of heaven, because he believes in material efficiency and unlimited com-petition, and that all men are born enemies,—and sees only their worst side and lowest motives. With him we reject the self-made man, because some generations must pass before the individual can cleanse himself from the earth that adheres after the struggle, —before the body can be perfectly formed and cared for and the mind freed from suspicion. " Nature's gentleman " is more true in theory than practice, and a good heart and a great mind by themselves suffice as little as the highest breeding without spiritual force.

We reject the poet because he rules by love only— for which the world is not ripe—and he cannot command men ; and we reject the real-politician—whether in affairs of state or business—whether he is Prussian Chancellor or Manchester or Chicago Captain of Industry —because he can only command. It is in heroic action— the General, the Statesman—that we discover our Master and Friend, and because he is both we wish him not to be perfect. The most fascinating pages of biography narrate its subject's personal habits, but it is falsely said that we spy out a great man's faults from envy. If the eye lights up and the attention quickens to read of Napoleon's rages, Wellington's love-affairs, Marl-borough's avarice, the debts of Chatham and Pitt,—it is that by their weaknesses they appear human as our selves. They reveal the Friend which we require as much as the Master to lead us from the City of Destruction and make us believe that the New Jerusalem is more than " an anxious wish, a great Perhaps."

Plutarch is our best instructor in hero-worship because he shows us human presence acting directly on the world : neither removed by the deep gulf of meditation of the Middle Ages nor the formulas and officialism of modern life : we shall see how Pompey fought a premature battle rather than disappoint his friends. We gave reasons for rejecting the self-made man, but as we open Plutarch and turn to the life of Marius, we realize, from his central episode, that in time of crisis only strength can save the world. He was born obscurely, and rose by hard work and self-denial, practising old Roman virtues, and, as General, delighting the soldiers by sharing their toils. But this, as well as the piteous wanderings of later years, and the blood-red sunset of the close, interest because they happened to him who hurled back the Cimbri and Teutones and saved Rome from the greatest danger that had ever threatened her. When news came that the barbarian host was advancing like the ocean, small respect was shown for members of noble families who proffered themselves for the command, and Marius was chosen as alone able to meet the tempest of so great a war. Then were forgotten his faults—that he never sacrificed to the Graces, or thought it worth while to learn Greek,—that he lacked " agreeableness of conversation," was ignorant of civil life, and only excelled in war. When he sued for the consulship and addressed the people, be belied his own character by striving to be popular and obliging ; his undaunted presence of mind in battle forsook him, and he was easily upset by praise or blame. But now that Rome must fight for her existence he was admired the more— if not loved—for his violent spirit, stern voice, and harsh aspect,—because these things would seem terrible to the enemy. He becomes greater as the reports of the foe become more awful : how they were terrible to look upon and uttered strange cries and shouts ; how, in crossing the Alps, they despised cold and fatigue, and slid down precipices on their shields. Marius wisely declined battle, and kept his soldiers within bulwarks till they were used to the sight of the barbarians,—and then fought and overcame, and triumphed. We think of this when he was driven from Rome by Sylla, and, treacherously put ashore by the sailors he had trusted, wades through marshes to a peasant's hut and begs on his knees to be saved. Even when fortune is again reversed, and he returns to Rome and commits unspeakable horrors, we still remember that once he was transfigured and like a god among men.

Another instance of the purely strong man is Cato
the Younger, who, unlike Marius, is morally strong.
He too was brought up austerely and cared nothing for
finer things, but, as a boy, was rough to those who
flattered him, and willed only justice. He despised
ornament either of dress or speech : while travelling
in Asia he sat on his own luggage, and, when prætor,
caused some scandal by coming to court without shoes.
Like Marius he was more soldier than officer, and the
affection that he won came unsought. All his life he
warred against corruption, and he lived at a time when
old Roman virtues were declining, the Republic tottering, and the death-grapple between Cæsar and Pompey
for absolute power impending over the city. The
transparently sincere man, devoted to justice, set in a
corrupt world, made no personal enemy. He was terrible
and severe in the senate and at the bar, yet after the
thing was over, his manner to all men was perfectly
friendly and humane. He had prosecuted Murena,
whom Cicero triumphantly defended, and Murena, when
consul, bore him no ill-will, and often asked him for
advice. Cæsar and Pompey honoured him : the latter,
when abroad, commended his wife and children to his
care ; and Cæsar, whom he had consistently opposed,
grudged him his death. When he saw in the manipu-
lated consular elections a conspiracy to subvert the
constitution and parcel out the empire, he supported
another candidate,—enduring blows and wounds, con-
tinuing to speak when pulled down by a serjeant, and
when forced out of the forum, returning again and again.
Having resolved to take his own life, he read Plato's
treatise on the soul, but he struck his slave violently for
removing his sword.

To compare the selfless Cato with the self-seeking
Marius, because both were simply strong men, may
seem absurd, but we must bear in mind that we are
awaiting an ideal hero. Both Marius and Cato were
heroes of a crisis, material in the first case, moral in the

second,—when earth is nearer to hell than heaven ; and the struggle for self-preservation, in nations as in men, is but the beginning of things. It might be fitter to compare Cato with Aristides whose devotion to justice was equally single-minded ; who served his country for no reward, and not only discarded riches but even glory ; who brought in his bills by other persons lest Themistocles should oppose him on principle ; who, when ostracised, prayed that Athens might never have occasion to remember him. There is something of the moral dawn with Cato, and sunset with Aristides : the one belongs to a world still young, the other to a world grown old. Aristides seems partly to decline worldly honours because he has inherited an older civilization and is nearer to the view-point that all is vanity. His one earthly tie was that he gloried in being poor, and we may parallel this with Cato's Platonic reading, and Marius's dying gesture—which recalls Bismarck—his complaint that he must die before he had attained his desire—which does show a stirring of the waters of the spirit, though foully mudded.

With Marcellus we move a stage upwards in Roman psychology—the man who could do and dare as bravely as the harshest, yet divined higher things. He admired Greek learning, and honoured those who excelled in it, though himself hindered by a life of fighting from completing his education. He took Syracuse, and wept to think that the rich and beautiful city must be made dismal and foul, but he dared not refuse the plunder to his army. Nothing affected him like the death of Archimedes, and he sought out and honoured his kindred. Till now Rome had ignored the arts, and refined persons shuddered at the city stuffed with barbarous arms and spoils stained with blood. Marcellus took back beautiful ornaments, and was even blamed by elder men for diverting the common people to vain and idle talk about curious things. He yielded to those who grudged him a third triumph, and, setting aside the " martial, terrible triumph," entered the city in ovation, wearing a garland of myrtle,—preferring to excite love and respect rather than fear. And yet, when charged by the Syracusans whom his enemies had brought over, he left his consul's curule chair and answered them like a private man, but struck greater consternation into their hearts by the power of his presence in his robe of state than in his armour.

There still clings to Marcellus something of early Rome, of the soul emerging like the sun rising in mists that blur its rays. Pompey announces a higher stage of culture, and he would be the ideal hero, but one greater is to follow ; and even so, being soft-mannered and iron-handed, he is greater than those heroes of the mind like Cicero and Brutus. The one lacked personal cour-age, the other knowledge of men, and so their great souls were mistakenly reflected in the earthly mirror. Pompey combined gentleness and dignity, and all through his career won from the Romans a devotion they had accorded to no other. As a mere youth he gained marvellous military successes all over the world, and triumphed before he was a senator. Though older men looked askance, he was given unlimited power to deal with the pirates, and in three months he scoured the seas, pardoning those that surrendered, and restoring them to civilized life, arguing that man is not wild by nature, but is made so by vicious habit, and may grow gentle again. Chosen to fight Mithridates, he was voluntarily raised to that absolute power which Sylla had won by force. He conquered as far as Syria and Judæa, and was no less famed for his justice than his might in arms. By his third triumph over Asia—his former were over Africa and Europe—he seemed to have led the whole world captive. Of more intimate things, we note that he charmed all, so that for his sake men endured his covetous and oppressive lieutenants ; that he was seduced by the vile Clodius to forsake Cicero, and, when the latter sought him, escaped by a back door ;

that he neglected public affairs to pass the time with his wife on whom he doted, and, when mocked by the people, took it ill because he was unused to hear anything disagreeable of himself ; that he favoured his friends in official matters. Meanwhile Cæsar grown famous in Gaulish wars, was intriguing and countermining, and the death of Crassus left the two face to face. When civil war broke out and Pompey left Rome, his conduct of the war was blamed, but he himself still loved. Having collected a splendid army, double that of Cæsar, he might have triumphed by biding his time, but he engaged battle prematurely because he could not bear reproach, or resist expectation of friends. So he fought and lost Pharsalia, and from lord of half the world became a fugitive,—to be done to death by assassins on the coast of Africa. Plutarch adds the harrowing touch, that his wife, from the ship, saw the small boat might not turn back, because the shore was covered with soldiers, and lamented for him as already dead.

Cæsar would not have escaped by back doors, or over-loved his wife, or been deflected by personal reasons for refusing battle. If he did greater things than Pompey it was because he made his heart serve his head. Pompey's human kindness flowed out upon the world ; Cæsar husbanded his emotional stream to turn the wheel of ambition. He assumed an affable manner to win popularity, and, when his young wife died, pronounced a funeral oration in her praise, against all precedent, so that people might regard him as tender-hearted. He spent ten years in conquering Gaul, and showed himself a commander second to none in history ; and he used the wealth which victory brought him to secure the favour of the Romans. Like an expert wrestler he trained himself and his army in Gaul for the duel with Pompey which the death of Crassus made inevitable. Before crossing the Rubicon and opening the flood-gates of civil war, we do find him meditating in human fashion over the calamities he would bring upon mankind, and the verdict of future generations ; and he shed tears at the tokens of Pompey's death. He pardoned, even honoured, many who had fought against him, thinking to found his power more safely on the people's love. We are more impressed by instances of Nelson's personal valour in combat than Napoleon's, because Nelson was human like Pompey, whereas Cæsar's daring is like that of Napoleon. Cæsar was small, spare, and epileptic, but he shrank from no danger or labour, and never made weakness an excuse for ease. When he fought in person against the Nervii and saved the battle, we recall how Napoleon, in his first Italian campaign, grasped a standard and led forward his wavering troops, or headed the rush upon the bridge swept by grape-shot. Even so we admire with reserve, because we feel that both used themselves and all men as means to the pre-determined end of exalting self. When Pompey fell, Cæsar could not live on his past, but struggled with himself as a rival, to eclipse his former actions by his future. He planned to march to Parthia and into Scythia and return by Germany and Gaul—in a vast curve, to bound his empire on all sides by the ocean : and he died because he wished to be king. " When that the poor have cried, Cæsar hath wept," spoke Shakespeare's Antony in the funeral oration. Shakespeare versified whole sentences and even paragraphs from his originals in the Roman plays, but we find nothing in Plutarch to correspond with this beautiful line.

Cæsar is Master, but not Master and Friend like Pompey, and yet perhaps the greatest Roman would be more fitly compared to the greatest Greek conqueror. Alexander pursued glory, and even feared that his father might conquer all before he had a chance, and when he could push his Indian expedition no further, prayed to the gods that no one might ever surpass him. He, too, shunned pleasures of sense and used his body hardly, but, unlike Cæsar, his mind reacted in a disinterested way to his human circle. He loved conversation, and

even indulged in boasting ; was a tender and anxious
friend ; and only became cruel when he heard someone
had spoken ill of him,—for he valued glory and reputation beyond life and kingdom. He permitted the sack
of Thebes and was afflicted by remorse throughout his
life. Cæsar, like Bismarck, preferred real to apparent
power, once observing that he would rather be the first
man in a village than second in Rome ; and we doubt
if he would have cared to know, in the world of shadows,
that it was his spirit which conquered at Philippi.

The Greek mind was a finer thing than the Roman,
and responded less immediately to the fact, because, in
the interval between stimulus and response, it had to
visit a larger circle of ideas. Cæsar did not fail morally
like Themistocles or Alcibiades, yet their unmoral
paths led them within sight of a region so far obscured
from every Roman but Pompey. To exalt self was their
prime object ; and we read of Alcibiades that he had
this peculiar talent and artifice for gaining men's affections,—that he could at once comply with and really
embrace and enter into their habits and ways of life, and
change faster than the chameleon, affecting either virtue
or vice as it pleased him : and, of Themistocles, that he
hoped never to sit on that tribunal where his friends
might not plead a greater privilege than strangers, Even
these crooked by-paths led them towards a country
impossible for the fair Roman highway. They saw,
though with earth-distracted vision, that the ultimate
reality is the communion of souls, not codes of laws and
principles made by man. The Roman mind worked
in a line to and from the fact, like the law of gravity ;
the Greek performed a fuller orbit because it let itself
be distracted by opinion and hearsay and wish to seem
something it was not. The Olympian Pericles wore a
pompous manner, and declined friendly visiting, because
a grave exterior is hardly maintained among friends,
and assumed superiority readily unmasked. Yet, having coaxed and flattered his countrymen with delights

and pleasures, like children, and bribed them with public moneys, and given Greece her public monuments,—when at last he had got all power into his hands, he became another man,—less tame and gentle with the populace,—though we read of no bloody proscriptions as at Rome, or armed men pouring into the Assembly. He led the people with their own consent, using his divine orator's gift, in Plato's words, to govern their souls by addressing the affections and passions,— prevailing even more by his character, being uncorrupted and indifferent to money. Whether his indifference in domestic trouble—abstaining from the funerals of his kindred—was real or assumed, we do not know ; but when his remaining son died, he was vanquished by grief as he crowned the corpse with a garland.

To mention Nicias after Pericles is like the moon compared to the sun, and his reserve lasted throughout his career. Too cautious to dine out or talk with his friends, hard of access, he won upon the people by seeming afraid of them. But the link between the two worlds—the Roman world of action, and the Greek world of action and imagination, is provided by the orators—Demosthenes and Cicero. Demosthenes went as ambassador through the Greek States, and by the power of his eloquence united them in a general league against Philip of Macedon. He prevailed even with the obstinate Thebans, so that Philip sent heralds to treat for peace. But he, once surrounded and courted by the commanders of all the armies, deserted his post in battle and threw away his arms. A similar lack of courage was charged against Cicero,—and in exile he appeared poor-spirited, humiliated, and dejected by his misfortunes. Even in speaking he began timidly and scarcely desisted from trembling when he was well launched into the current of his speech. When he defended Milo, the sight of troops encamped round the Forum and the glitter of arms so unnerved him, that he could hardly begin his speech because his body shook

and tongue halted. Yet he approaches the Greek nearer
than Pompey or Brutus, the two other finest Roman
minds. It was not public indifference that abated his
early ambition, but the thought that the glory he con-
tended for was an infinite thing, and there was no fixed
end nor measure in its pursuit. Yet he always delighted
in hearing himself praised, even offending people by
praising himself ; and he did to others as he would
himself be done by, never inflicting punishment with
reproach on those under his command, never in his anger
using words that hurt, causing no one to be beaten.
Even when he saved Rome by unmasking Catiline, who
designed to massacre the senate and others and fire the
city, having allotted hundreds to kindle fire and stop
the aqueducts,—he hesitated to inflict death. It is a
trait to be noted that on his second journey to Greece
he visited the friends of his youth ; and we well believe
that the feud with Antony sprang from the difference
of their manners. The circumstances of Pompey's fate
are repeated in a fashion yet more ghastly, because it is
a finer head that falls. We hold our breath while his
servants, divided in their counsels, hurry him this way
and that in his litter, till, betrayed by the youth he had
educated, he himself commands the litter to be set down
in the shady walks and turns his grief-worn face upon
the assassins.

Among the morally great is Brutus, who was loved by
all and not even hated by his enemies. No flattery
could prevail on him to hear an unjust petition : he
spared himself no labour, was insensible of the passions
of anger, pleasure, covetousness,—and inflexible to
maintain his purpose for what he thought right and
honest. He exceeds Cato because he added learning
and philosophy to a good disposition, and would employ
his spare time in camp in reading and study, even the day
before a battle.

But the moralist's reward is not in this world, and we
are seeking an earthly king. Brutus pleases less than

Pompey, but we promised to touch a greater life than
Pompey's, and the reader of Plutarch will be half shocked
to hear that we put forward Antony. Not that his faults
are forgotten : his early ostentatious, vaunting temper,
full of empty flourishes and unsteady efforts for glory,—
his drinking-bouts at all hours, his wild expenses, his
gross amours, the day spent in sleeping or walking off
his debauches, the night in revelling with buffoons. On
his journeys, he quartered loose women and singing girls
on the houses of serious fathers and mothers of families ;
he deprived persons of worth and quality of their fortunes
to gratify villains and flatterers ; once he gave his cook
the house of a Magnesian citizen as a reward for a
single successful supper. But even these are trifles
compared to his share in what Plutarch calls the cruellest
transaction that had ever taken place—the proscriptions
that followed his reconciliation with Octavius, when they
exchanged blood for blood, and his first victim was
Cicero. Nay more, at the sight of Cicero's severed head
and hand, he burst out in laughter, and caused them to
be hung over his place in the forum. Yet we are told
that Cæsar by dealing gently with his errors did much
to cure him ; that in misfortune he was most nearly
a virtuous man ; that he endured incredible hardships
in crossing the Alps, drinking foul water and eating
wild roots, sharing the tasks of the common soldiers,
and inspiring a personal devotion in them beyond any
other Roman general. He was simple, and ignorant of
things done in his name, and when his faults were pointed
out, he repented sincerely and asked pardon : as when
told that Asia had raised two hundred thousand talents
for his service. He was not subtle enough to see that
persons who spoke out boldly were parasites ; though sharp
of tongue himself, he accepted repartee with good humour;
and he made friends of persons by helping them in their
love affairs. It was Cicero's bitter speeches, telling the
people details of his gross pleasures, and denouncing him
as author of the civil war, that cut him to the quick.

Such marks of sensitiveness would not have condoned his vices and cruelties but for the crowning episode of his life—his love of Cleopatra. Antony was an artist, but, being also general, statesman, orator, he could shape the world to his wish and build his whole life into a poem. His ill deeds—bestowing a citizen's property on a jester who had pleased him for the moment—show a great spirit overlooking material considerations. Haunted by a vision of beauty, it was natural that he should see it in a woman's form, Because earth was mixed with heaven he was no Platonic lover, and because heaven was mixed with earth he neglected external things, as the poet may but the man of affairs may not. To pass the winter with Cleopatra he pushed on a war before its due time, and once put off war with the Parthians when they were disabled by internal disputes. He let Cleopatra over-rule him to fight at sea at Actium, though his navy was weaker than the enemy and his army stronger ; and, when the issue hung doubtful, because Cleopatra took fright and fled, he followed and abandoned all who were fighting and dying for him. In the last scene, as life ebbs from the self-inflicted wound, the flame of the spirit burns clear, and he bids her not pity but rejoice for him in remembrance of his past happiness.

He is above Cæsar, above the just Cato and the juster Brutus, even above Pompey and the finer-minded Greeks—Pericles who gave Athens beautiful monuments unsurpassed to-day—Alexander who conquered to India but respected his royal women captives, esteeming it more kingly to govern himself than conquer his enemies. What we noted in passing of Pompey and Themistocles and Alcibiades is fully expressed by Antony. He saw the individual as the centre of life, and, the fates having granted him world-power, he expended nations' treasuries and put battles aside for the individual's sake. To him most of all pagans, heaven was revealed in the individual soul, and he dismissed moral systems and codes of laws and armies and kingdoms as secondary matters. His religion, like the poet's, had much of sense, yet he attained the last truth : that the great soul, expressed by the perfect form, is God's deputy on earth, whose commands must be obeyed, whether or not they overturn the established order of the world.

Antony did not crush the individual like Cæsar, prefer causes and abstract justice like Brutus, or escape by a back door like Pompey ; though he might forswear himself and promise the same thing to two persons ; and we know that he listened impatiently to petitions. But because he never overlooked the individual, the power of his presence reacted equally upon the world, and he is the Master and Friend. Twice he stopped an army in flight and re-gained victory, and he kindled such love in the soldiers that they set his good opinion above their lives. When Actium sealed his doom he entreated his friends to leave him, comforted them with all imaginable goodness and humanity, and offered them a treasure-ship, which they refused with tears. He was noble and eloquent, with frank and open manners and liberal and magnificent habits, familiar in talk with everybody, and he pitied and helped the sick. Once in Asia, kings waited at his door, and queens rivalled one another to make him the greatest presents or appear most charming in his eyes. He was a magnificent man, with well-grown beard, large forehead, aquiline nose, and bold masculine look that suggested Hercules.

We have found our Master and Friend, but before leaving Plutarch we will moor his galley of heroes alongside a northern quay and suffer a modern figure to step down among them. Can it be that the fire of genius in their eyes burns dimmer, and their facial lines look simpler by contrast ? Between the fifth and fifteenth centuries man found his soul, but the stress of modern life exacted that he should re-materialize himself and acquire a neo-pagan character. The process was one of pain, for he had to reckon with the resisting power of his deepest self,—and the result is writ large in his tortured countenance.

We will turn to the world's third greatest biographer —assuming Plutarch and Boswell to hold the first places —and study Carlyle's portrait of Frederick William, maker of modern Prussia, and father of Frederick the Great. It was he who realized that fear of God would no longer deter nations from preying upon each other, and that if a nation grew rich without a perfectly drilled army, that nation would perish—more especially his own which had no natural frontiers. That he thought truly the sequel proved, when, after Austria's defeat at Mollwitz, all the Powers except England repudiated Pragmatic Sanction. As Crown Prince he had understood that the army was the heart and pith of Prussia, and as king he sacrificed all to make it efficient. It became his life-business to shape Prussia after his own image—into a thrifty, hardy, rigorous, and Spartan country. He reduced the royal household to the lowest footing of the indispensable, cutting down things to below the fifth ; he went through every department of Prussian business, requiring needful work to be rigorously well done, and imaginary work pitched out of doors. He saved money yearly and deposited it in barrels in his Castle cellars. He drilled not only the army but the whole nation, striking loungers over the head with his cane, and not letting even Apple-women sit without knitting. He had bogs drained, colonies planted, manufactures established ; he reared tight human dwellings on what were once scraggy waste places. His recruiting methods cast an anxious shadow over the whole rural population.

And yet this king, of short, firm stature, with severe eyes and nasal voice, a harsh master and almost half mad, was sensitive as a poet or a woman. How severely he struggled to subdue his soul and organize his world to be materially efficient only, we can see from his relations with his son. Frederick William was German to the core ; the son craved for those Athenian-French delicacies which the father had swept from his Court. The Prince—afterwards to be Frederick the Great— disliked soldiering and hunting, and instead of joining in sow-baiting, would retire into a glade and play the flute with his friends, or converse with Mamma and her ladies. The King had commanded the Prince's tutors to infuse in him a true love of soldiering, and forbidden him to learn Latin or lingo of old dead heathens. How the Prince let his blond locks grow in Versailles fashion, how he read fiction, how he shut himself up with a Latin instructor, and how the King burst in and smote down on the instructor with his cane : all this is written in Carlyle's great chapters.

Carlyle rightly divined the King to be sensitive as a poet or woman, and also rightly describes him as a terrible king or father. The anger of a materialized person is terrible, because the laws of his world are beyond doubt. In the spiritual world we can prove nothing.—neither that God exists nor that our friends love us ; but we detect the bungler in an army manœuvre, or the mason who builds a house that is not rain-proof. No doubt the King read rightly the signs of the times,— that if the army failed, his country was lost, and was therefore deaf to the warning against care and advice to take no thought for the morrow. The sceptical eighteenth century turned love to fear in the hearts of many, and because fear is the cruellest passion, and this King had a deep soul, the result appears in his unhappy household and apprehensive subjects. Christianity had taught men to sacrifice this world to another ; and neo-pagan- ism, or the cult of material efficiency, likewise required continuous self-denial. But the disharmony was that the fears and anxieties stored by the soul through the watches of the long night of the Middle Ages were expended upon temporal things. Like the business man who despises all but money-making. Frederick William spent his life in fortifying himself against every imaginable mischance. There are times when the soul does break through the hard earthly crust, at the cost of pain that mortal man can scarcely bear : these are when the road of life leads near the Valley of the Shadow. When the Queen fell ill and was in danger, he was like to break his heart ; and when George I died, and no one else cared, he wept tenderly for the uncle who had been good to him as a boy. His heart did all but break when his son, whom he had ill-treated, planned to fly : nevertheless he condemned him as a Colonel who had tried to desert ; and his accomplice—the unfortunate Katte—had indeed to die. We think of the King's grief and remember how Antony enjoyed killing Cicero and insulted the mortal remains ; but in the interval man's soul had gone down to hell and ascended again to heaven. But if it needed the stimulus of death to make Frederick William doubt whether this outer world which so troubled him was indeed a real thing, how much more when his own hour struck, and he had to leave behind him the twin supports of well-drilled army and full treasury and walk the plank of his life-vessel alone ! The materialized and angry man became his true self—the womanly-sensitive poet. He would bear no faces about his sick bed except those he liked, and he feared to be left alone with the clergyman who reminded him of certain tyrannous acts he had committed. As for the next world, he doubted it no more than Potsdam and the giant grenadiers.

But as our theme is Plutarch let us end with Plutarch and measure the parting gulf by re-comparing Frederick William with the Roman whom he most resembled—Marcus Cato—known as Cato the Censor. He too placed frugality and temperance above all the virtues, and was more famed for his simple life than his eloquence. When consul he drank the same wine as his workmen, and eschewed handsome slaves in favour of the able and sturdy, reckoning nothing superfluous a good bargain. The humane Plutarch blames him for taking the work out of his servants as out of brute beasts, and turning them off and selling them in their old age,—as if there should be no further commerce between man and man than what brings profit. He regretted all his life that he had once spent a day without doing any business of moment. He wished to be censor because it enabled him to enquire into everyone's life and manners : and having attained the office, he threatened evil livers, retrenched people's luxury, and assessed luxurious things at ten times their worth, to increase the taxes on them. He would have approved the Prussian King's choice of wooden furniture only, to avoid dust. As Frederick William excluded Latin from practical education, and banished Wolf because he was told his philosophy might subvert discipline in the army, and derived the trouble with his son from foreign books,—so Cato despised philosophy, scoffed at Greek studies, and pronounced like an oracle that Greek literature would destroy Rome. In each was the same conscious dumb ignorance of all things beyond his own small horizon of personal survey. Cato wrote a book on country matters, and Frederick William's semi-articulate writings on economics were as if done by the paw of a bear. As Frederick William dreaded the ring of potential foes round Prussia, so Cato's saying, " Carthage must be destroyed," became a proverb.

But we look on Cato's grim countenance and reflect that it cost him no pains to be himself. He excused his avaricious humour, and affirmed that he was a wonderful, nay, a godlike man, who left more behind him than he had received : whereas in Frederick William was much internal modesty, self-distrust, anxiety. Both lived outer lives, but Frederick William had to forget the Middle Ages and his soul. Cato would thrust his " Carthage must be destroyed " into every debate in the senate, whether occasion fitted or no, but he was never haunted in his sleep by Carthaginian terrors and imaginings, and he did not suspect his son of conniving with his country's enemies, and bully and strike him. In the pagan world man was responsible to men ; in the Middle Ages to God ; the perils of the modern world have distracted man from God and forced him to acquire a neo-pagan character,—to deny his soul and forsake his brother : and how agonising that process may be we learn from this extreme instance.

George Borrow

GEORGE BORROW

WHEN the *Life of Borrow*, by Dr. Knapp, appeared in 1899, the *Spectator* hazarded the doubt whether there still remained persons who took interest in his works. For nearly a decade after this lugubrious comment the silence was unbroken. In 1908, however, came Mr. Walling's book ; and a significant feature of the years that followed was the inclusion of Borrow's works in the countless reprints of standard authors that were pouring from the press. In 1912 were published two further biographies ; and in July, 1913, the newspapers gave prominence to the celebrations in his honour at Norwich. Later still appeared Mr. Clement Shorter's *George Borrow and his Circle*, which again emphasized the ephemeral nature of his success with the *Bible in Spain* in 1843, and the complete oblivion by the public which he suffered thereafter.

Borrow has been described as a cross between Carlyle and Sir Richard Burton, with a touch of the Brontës. It is not easy to trace any resemblance to the last, save that he was of Celtic parentage and had the Celtic melancholy and foreboding habit. His simple and natural style is as unlike theirs as indeed it is to Carlyle's. It reveals nothing of the mental agitation of *Villette* and the *Latter-Day Pamphlets*. Yet apart from the form of his writings there are some notable points of resemblance to Carlyle, in the violence of his splenetic outbursts, the ruggedness of his personality, and his failure to find happiness in the practice of his art. The beauty of

Borrow's domestic life forbids the further analogy that he was " gey ill to live with " [1] ; yet it was characteristic of him that he never admitted his own dog to be in the wrong when that quadruped entered the lists with a neighbour's. The prejudices of both men were the effect of outraged sensibility. Carlyle took life with terrible seriousness and had stern ideals of what man should be ; yet among his friends were certain unstrenuous persons. One of them was Leigh Hunt, his neighbour in Chelsea, the reason for their friendship being the interchange of courtesies that neighbourhood allows ; and Carlyle's crust of ill nature melted at the touch of personal kindness. Borrow's last years were spent in almost total seclusion from the world, because the decline of his reputation placed him, as he thought, at a disadvantage. It was the sensitiveness of his youth renewed, when, having failed on his first journey to London to find a publisher for his ballads, he feared to return to Norwich lest people should inquire after their fate. Both Borrow and Carlyle had the " soft " temperament, which, as Lord Morley once said, is " easily agitated," and the disturbance, although it does not cause " true anger or lasting indignation, sends quick currents of eager irritation along the sufferer's nerves."

As Burton's writings are not high art, comparison would be unfruitful ; but the lives of the two men present points of close similarity. In both a desultory education fostered a love of wandering, for which enormous physical strength and indomitable courage fitted them. Burton loved to disguise himself, Borrow to affect mystery, and assume that he knew all and was known of none. And yet both had the simplicity of character which, alone among great men, Macaulay denied to the elder Pitt. They lacked the facile pessimism of the man of the world as much as his worldly

[1] Fuller acquaintance with Carlyle's story has shown how Froude misapplied this phrase.

wisdom. It appears in Burton's tenure of the Damascus consulship, his relations with Speke, and his failure to visit England on the conclusion of his journey to Mecca, when the country was ringing with his fame ; while Borrow consumed his youth in translating Danish ballads, hoping to win thereby permanent reputation : in contrast to his astute colleague Bowring, who pursued the same task solely as a means to secure a consular appointment.

Borrow was half man of action and half poet. It is from action that his imaginative force derives ; and although he failed as a maker of verse, and his fame rests upon four volumes of prose, the cast of his mind was poetic ; the intellectual yields to the emotional. The effect of weak reasoning powers on the main course of his life is but too apparent. It led him into many a blind alley of effort, and retarded the development of his powers. He was neither indolent nor lacked per-severance nor concentration—three shortcomings which before now have withheld success from gifted men or deferred it till late in life. At school he was considered of less than average ability : although there is no authority for the statement, it is possible that he learnt his Euclid by heart. As a youth, his father pronounced him unfitted for any profession ; and, being placed in a solicitor's office, he neglected the law and mastered the Welsh language. And yet his philological studies were without scientific groundwork ; he acquired languages because he had a prodigious memory for words, and, following the line of least resistance, he imposed the whole tax upon his memory. He failed as a hack author in London, and, with his usual love of mystification, created the legend of the "veiled period," so as to disguise from the public the sordid actualities of his seven lean years ; and to this period, in after life, he liked reference as little as did Dr. Johnson to that preceding 1755, when the publication of the Dictionary made his circumstances easy. The growth of experience and comparison of past failures, rather than reason, taught him what kind of pains to take ; and the accident of his appointment to the Bible Society provided the circumstances which gave his powers full play.

The years which Borrow passed in Spain, as agent to the Society, were perhaps the happiest in his life. They supplied the constant change, for lack of which in after years his nature languished and black thoughts swarmed in his mind. To think, with Borrow, was an infallible sign of disease ; his metaphysical questionings display a mind moving in a circle ; they are the outcome of overstrained energies in unfavourable surroundings rather than philosophic thirst for knowledge. He admitted himself that he was ill qualified to argue : the question, What is Truth ? puzzled him as much as its first propounder. He could never see more than a balance of probabilities, and like many persons with the artistic temperament, he was morbidly sensitive to sugges- tion. He surrendered his faith without a struggle to the attacks of William Taylor of Norwich, and one of his projects, on first visiting London at the age of twenty-one to try his fortunes as an author, was to " abuse religion." Small wonder that his subsequent connection with the Bible Society evoked, in the words of Harriet Martineau, " one shout of laughter from all who remembered the old Norwich days." There is no mention in Dr. Knapp's pages of the renascence of Borrow's faith, but doubtless it is explained by this sentence of *Romany Rye :* " For a long time I doubted the truth of Scripture, owing to certain conceited dis- courses which I had heard from certain conceited individuals, but now I begin to believe firmly." It was the change of circumstances which, restoring him to the wandering life for which he was fitted, and removing him from the argumentative sphere for which he was unfitted, established the harmonious functioning of his powers.

Borrow's first mission in the service of the Bible Society

was to St. Petersburg. It occupied him for two years, and on his return he wrote thus to his mother : " I hope the Society will employ me upon something new, for I have of late led an active life, and dread the thought of having nothing to do except studying as formerly, and I am by no means certain that I could sit down to study now. I can do anything if it is to turn to any account——" The Society responded to his appeal by despatching him to Spain, where he spent four years in circulating the Scriptures among the benighted peasantry.

The artistic temperament without the artistic faculty is perhaps the heaviest burden that can be laid upon mortal man ; yet so puissant is the glamour of great art that even the minor poet—in the event of reincarnation—would choose to be his ineffectual self again and see the glorious world go by in the distance rather than walk through life as a Philistine : unlike Odysseus in the vision of Er, who, disenchanted of ambition, was left to the last in his search for the lot of a private man without cares. Till the age of thirty-two, Borrow's nature had been perplexed by the need for expression. and found no adequate relief. Now, less from reasoned choice than necessity, he struck the right path. The *Gypsies of Spain*, his first notable work, which stands midway between the undistinguished poetry and the four books on which his fame rests, was composed as he travelled, " in ventas and posadas " ; and the letters, expressed in literary form, which he wrote to the Bible Society, were subsequently reshaped into the *Bible in Spain*, which scored a phenomenal success in 1843.

The unique nature of his experiences may have ensured the immediate success of Borrow's book, but the emotional content gave it permanent value. Richard Ford, author of a once famous book on Spain, advised Borrow to eschew poetry and descriptions of scenery and give exciting facts ; and Borrow partially complied. But there is an interest transcending that of incident and adventure. It arises from his power to annihilate himself in the presence of strange people and strange places, to make of his mind a white sheet whereon to receive impressions.

Borrow acknowledged Defoe to be his master ; the reading of *Robinson Crusoe* first thawed the ice which bound his mind as a child. Watts-Dunton described both as masters of the " psychological kind of autobiographic fiction." Defoe heightens the interest in the adventures it was his primary object to describe by " humanising " them, by " making it appear that they worked a great life-lesson for the man who experienced them." But the *Bible in Spain* has not that fear of danger to the central figure which makes parts of *Robinson Crusoe* agonizing. How pitiful is the scene where Crusoe is all but swept out to sea in his attempt to circumnavigate the island, and when the place which had once seemed to him a horrible desert now appears to contain all the happiness his heart could wish for. How haunting are his reflections upon his false security in the years before he knew that his island was the resort of cannibals, when perhaps the brow of a hill or the casual approach of night had come between him and the worst kind of destruction. Conversely, when Borrow is fired upon by the Portuguese soldiers, we think less of his peril than of the perpetrators of the outrage,—the villainous-looking ruffians, their livid and ghastly countenances, where murder is written, and their harsh, croaking voices. And it is the same of his sojourn in the Madrid prison.

The centre of interest is what Borrow sees and what he suffers for others, as he goes to and fro in once mighty Spain, whence the glory has departed ; crossing and recrossing its wild moors, climbing its flinty hills, threading the passes of its stupendous mountain-chains, and sojourning in strange inns. The mysterious attracts him in nature as in man, as when he dwells upon the caves or " midnight abysses " of Gibraltar, the depths of which no one has fathomed, while numbers have lost their lives in the attempt.

Together with this interest is that of the strange people with whom he consorted. The intense sympathy revealed by Borrow for beings of the vagrant class has led to the false assertion that he cared only for " blackguard speci-mens of humanity " ; and the *Saturday Review*, with characteristic loss of temper, entitled its article on his Life and Letters in 1899, " A Sordid Hero." Like Wordsworth, Borrow disliked complex natures, and also his sensitiveness hindered that annihilation of self in intercourse with his equals without which the mind is not set free to consider another's point of view. In colloquy with the world's outcasts, or with the mortally wounded in the battle of life—with all who did not watch and criticize—there was nothing to stem the rich flow of sympathy from mind to mind. When he visits the Archbishop of Toledo, conversation languishes till allusion to a brilliant on the Prelate's finger gives it a fillip ; but words do not fail him in the presence of Benedict Moll. His treatment of strollers and vaga-bonds may be contrasted rather than compared with that of Dickens. With Borrow there is a simple transmigra-tion of his soul into their bodies ; with Dickens a thou-sand threads attach them to their creator, and the coloured beams of his fancy cease not to play upon them through all their antics. It is in Wordsworth that the same quality of self-abnegation where the sympathies are enlisted, will be found : in such a poem as the *Reverie of Poor Susan*, among a host that rise to the mind. Both writers had a ready ear for a tale of distress, and a simplicity of character which gave it lyric rather than dramatic utterance. " That you are no impostor I feel convinced," said Borrow to Benedict Moll, the infatuated treasure-seeker, when warning him of the fate that befalls impostors. In the Madrid prison was a French convict, shortly to be garotted, who had served in Napoleon's Russian campaign, and plied his trade of

robber in the Landes, yet he summed up his life as
containing " nothing remarkable." Borrow writes :
" I looked him in the face and spoke to him, but he did
not seem either to hear or see me. His mind was
perhaps wandering in that dreadful valley of the shadow,
into which the children of earth, whilst living, occasionally
find their way." The picturesque setting of these incidents entitles Borrow to comparison with an author
far removed in age and race, and the master of the most
winning and gracious style in the whole of literature.
The anecdotes with which the history of Herodotus is
interspersed—such as Crœsus and Solon, Cleobis and
Bito, Polycrates—may be set side by side with those of
Benedict Moll, Judah Lib, and the crone of Merida.
But the persons in Herodotus are the puppets of fate ;
in Borrow they are possessed by an idea—the pursuit of
wealth, of revenge, of lost kindred—which drives them
to their doom.

Two of the most characteristic incidents are the ride
with the gypsy Antonio, and the journey to Finisterra ;
and it might be profitable to glance at them as illustrat-
ing Borrow's peculiar power of blending strange persons
and places. The first speaks of days spent on wild
moors strewn with rocks, of descents into ruinous and
deserted towns, of narrow lanes and a dilapidated house,
where in a large, dark room dusky figures crouch over
a brasero ; of the journey renewed over the savage
moor, of the dismal town and the low, mean hut where
no answer is returned to a knock. In the second, Borrow
relates how it was his wish to proceed to Finisterra to
leave there a single Testament, because the ship which
carried him to Spain had nearly been dashed to pieces
against " the rocky sides of this extreme point of the
Old World." Having with difficulty procured a guide
to a place so wild and remote, he sets out over flinty
hills and through stony ravines. The guide appears to
be half-witted, and when they are benighted on a moor,
he informs Borrow that so far from knowing the road

to Finisterra, he disbelieves in the existence of such a place ; and he is fearful of the spirits of the dead who haunt the wildest heath of the wildest province in Spain, and ride upon the haze, bearing candles. They pass the night in a Gallegan hut as guests of a man who had never slept in a bed in his life. Resuming their journey, they come within sight of the bold coastline. It was such a place as Borrow had conceived in his youth, " the termination of the world, beyond which there was a wild sea or abyss or chaos." " Such is the grave," he exclaims, " and such are its terrific sides." They have been warned not to venture among " the drunkards of Finisterra," who may play them a trick, but they advance along the winding and deserted street. Eyes peer at them through the chinks of walls. They tie up the horse in what they believe to be the stable of an inn ; it is at once untied and driven forth. They ascend the huge bluff and gaze out upon the " wilderness of waters." Then Borrow returns to the inn and falls asleep. From troubled dreams he is violently wakened to behold an uncouth figure hanging over him in the light of the descending sun. We may repeat what Victor Hugo said of Baudelaire, that he had added " a new shudder " to literature. Or it affects us as our childish minds were affected by a well-remembered passage in Grimm's Fairy Tales, of how a wanderer saw in strange countries persons with horns and beaks.

The world which Borrow creates by this fusion of action and imagination is not a world of realities, neither is it the interpenetration of the real and unseen—the light that never was on sea or land, but rather that middle region between the two, the world of dreams. The *Bible in Spain* was compiled from genuine letters, and is by no means a work of fiction, but it never saw the light as a book till it had received the finishing touches of Borrow's subconscious mind.

It was characteristic of Borrow that his next work was determined by the suggestions of admirers of the

Bible in Spain. As that work neared completion he had exclaimed more than once, " Alas ! what shall I do when it is finished ? " He had exhausted his adventures, and it was not in him to invent scenes or characters or depict manners. In vain his friend Hasfeldt wrote : " Your life is at present just what we talked of so often in bygone days. You wanted to live in the country a quiet, easy life——" Neither the happiness of his marriage, the ease of his circumstances, or his fame as an author could compensate the wanderer for lost liberty. From a condition of restlessness and melancholy he was roused by the request of friends to prefix a short account of himself to the *Bible in Spain,* to gratify the curiosity of readers. It inspired him to write the five volumes of autobiography published as *Lavengro* and *Romany Rye* in 1851 and 1857. Their failure, and the extinction of his reputation during his lifetime was due partly to misunderstanding by his public, and partly to his own unwisdom in abruptly terminating *Lavengro* and postponing for six years the conclusion of the story of Isopel Berners.

The popular objection to *Lavengro* was its mingling of fact and fiction. The cry arose, " This is very wonderful, if true ; but if fiction, it is pointless." At the present day we have the facts of Borrow's life in our possession, and can discriminate between historical and imaginative truth. When Professor Bradley published his *Oxford Lectures on Poetry,* in 1909, the *Athenæum* described him as of the receptive school of criticism, by contrast with the active school of Matthew Arnold. His method was to judge by the impressions left on the reader's mind, that of Arnold, to " block out widely " his author's distinctive merits and assess their value by comparison with the achievements of others. (Yet it was Arnold who selected from the world's great poets half-a-dozen surpassing lines for the student to commit to memory and use as a touchstone in future reading.) An opinion not begot of an impression is like a house with no foundation ; the response given by the reader's impressions is the final court of appeal. It is thus hard to believe that Borrow's contemporaries accused him of writing an " unveracious autobiography," and that this reflected back upon the *Bible in Spain* and weakened their faith in it. *David Copperfield* is a blending of fact and fiction, but we do not less enjoy two of its most humorous episodes, the fight with the young butcher, and the flirtation with Miss Larkins, because they are mythical.

It is ill-fitting to apply to permanent literature the same tests as to the latest novel which creates a *furore* because of its heroine's likeness to some well-known social figure. We are not now disposed to quarrel with Borrow because he provided bad gossip for his contemporaries ; our task is to pass by those portions of the edifice which are built of perishable bricks, and seek the temples wrought with the old Egyptian secret where stones are laid upon each other and no join may be perceived. The con-temners of *Lavengro* were like the ancient unbelievers who clamoured for a sign, or the modern ones who demand of science objective proof of a ruler of the universe, who wish to believe without believing, and to attain faith apart from spiritual experience.

We readily believe Borrow's statement in the *Gypsies of Spain* that he remembers no period when the mention of the word gypsy " did not awaken feelings in his mind hard to be described, but in which a strange pleasure predominated," because of a passage like the following, where, speaking of the time when gypsies were first seen in Europe, he dispels the false legend that Egypt was their home, whence they were banished for having denied hospitality to the Virgin and her child : " It probably originated amongst the priests and learned men of the East of Europe, who, startled by the sudden apparition of bands of people foreign in appearance and language, skilled in divination and the occult arts, endeavoured to find in Scripture a clue to such a phe-nomenon." The test of a true emotion in the author is the sympathetic thrill which its expression evokes in the reader ; and here the words do their work like the pollen which the bee carries from flower to flower for the process of fertilization.

The confusion between historical and imaginative truth has encouraged the young writer to believe that there is a royal road from the base of Parnassus to its topmost rock. Mr. J. W. Mackail has first uttered the truth that " all poetry is artificial, and the greatest poetry that of the most consummate artifice " ; and it was well remarked that " bad poets can be very confidential." Otherwise, the handbooks assure us that " sincerity is genius " ; and the giants of expression, secure in their command of the creative faculty, abet them. Carlyle exclaims that " he that speaks what is really in him, will find men to listen, though under never such impediments " ; Emerson, that " he that writes to himself writes to an eternal public " ; and Milton's muse dictates to him " easy his unpremeditated verse." In his early writings Lord Morley animadverted with insistence upon the folly of those writers who secluded themselves from the world : as if war and politics had created the genius of Thucydides and Voltaire. Without going so far as Mr. Arthur Symons, who limits Scott's output of genuine poetry to *Proud Maisie*, a song of sixteen lines, we can safely say that no experience, whether inward or outward, can effect that ultimate mastery over words which is creation. Take Shelley's famous lines :

> " Most wretched men
> Are cradled into poetry by wrong,
> They learn in suffering what they teach in song,"

and place beside them the couplet with which George Eliot concludes her sonnet-sequence, *Brother and Sister :*

> " But were another childish world my share,
> I would be born a little sister there,"

and we see how sincerity and depth of feeling have all but done the work of the true faculty. Shelley has piled his offering on the altar and fire from heaven has come down to consume it ; George Eliot has deftly placed hers to catch the rays of the sunset and deceive us with a mimic conflagration.

Prose being a more diffused art than poetry, this is true of it in a modified form ; and it behoves the reader who follows the windings of Borrow's mind in *Lavengro* and *Romany Rye* to select those passages which have the transmuting touch. And who cannot discriminate between such characters as the publisher and the old apple-woman on London Bridge ? Both episodes are true, but the publisher speaks like a third-rate actor, while of the apple-woman we hear the authentic voice. Yet a first perusal of *Lavengro* does leave upon the mind an impression of commonplace. It inclines us to echo the strictures of its contemporary reviewers, that a life of adventure had been unproductive of wisdom and reflection. And even when closer study has revealed the underlying earnestness, we still regret that the autobiography as a whole is not more intensive.

It appears as if Borrow transcribed his life with its succeeding episodes in the simplest language and without comment. He recalls objects that pleased the child rather for their happy associations than their play on an unfolding mind. His first acquaintance with *Robinson Crusoe* is alone touched with that awe with which those who re-live their youth in imagination approach mental landmarks. Borrow's philosophy may be summed up in the phrase that " circumstances are destiny." The famous John Newton saw a man on his way to be hanged, and exclaimed, " There goes John Newton, but for the grace of God ! " And so there is no special pleading in Borrow's narrative, no futile regrets for the past, but a spirit of necessitarianism which marks off his work from others of its kind. He is not bowed beneath a load of sins like Bunyan, neither has he the self-complacency of Gibbon. There is not the impassioned regret of St. Augustine for a vicious youth, or Newman's anxiety to explain his position to the world. How different are the tears he sheds on the banks of the Tweed because it is haunted ground, and those of Rousseau because he is declining into the vale of years and has not known love !

All his life Borrow had been exercised in mind on the subject of crime and virtue, especially during the period of authorship in London when he helped to compile the *Newgate Lives*, and at the time of his sojourn in the prison at Madrid. In the latter place was the son of a murderer, a boy of seven, much petted and fondled by the other prisoners. He writes : " What an enigma is this world of ours ! How dark and mysterious are the sources of what is called crime and virtue ! If that infant wretch became eventually a murderer like his father, is he to blame ? " So it is not surprising that he re-travels his own road as he remembers it, with no deepening of shadows from a fuller experience. Once, writing of his father, he says : " I who was so little like thee that thou understood'st me not, and in whom with justice thou didst feel so little pride, had yet perception enough to see all thy worth, and to feel it an honour to be able to call myself thy son." But even this wistful sentence is less charged with self-reproach than we might expect. He tells how the servant describes him as a child weak *here*, pointing to her forehead ; how his father misdoubts his fitness for any profession ; how he consumed his youthful leisure in learning strange languages and associating with strange people. He admits to sadly misspending his time, and to have always misspent it, " but could I, taking all circumstances into consideration, have done better than I had ? " It is seldom that Lavengro interrupts his stepping westward to look back. When he leaves London ; when he starts at the reflection of his face in the water because it is squalid and miserable ; when he goes to church where he had last been as an innocent child, and now he had become a moody man : these are some of his departures from neutrality. Had *Lavengro* been a drama, the scene of its prologue would have been laid in heaven, and the actions of its characters predetermined once and for ever.

It is a passionless atmosphere that recalls the Limbo pictured by Dante where the heathen poets dwell without joy or sorrow. There is some justification for an earlier critic's remark that *Lavengro* is a portfolio of sketches. The characters do not revolve round the central figure and possess varying degrees of attraction for each other. They move in solitary orbits with their attendant moons, and on not all of them is there life.

When Borrow does depart from his necessitarian method and meditates on cause and effect, it is a sign of disease. He was a born wanderer, and his mental and bodily health depended on change of scene and un-tainted air. The period of authorship in London shook his constitution to its foundations, and aimless question-ings such as this would escape him : " Will a time come when all will be forgotten that now is beneath the sun ? If so, of what profit is life ? " It is the cry of a mind the edge of which has been worn down by work for which it is unfitted. He must have felt that most painful of all reactions from brain exercise : the same weariness and lassitude on sitting down to begin his task as if he had toiled at it for hours. He left London and took to the roads because his mind was sick and he feared consumption. He could not, in the words of Musset,

> " ——vivre entre deux murs et quatre faces mornes,
> Le front sous un moellon, les pieds sur un tombeau."

And no sooner does the roar of the great city grow faint than Lavengro comes to his own and his powers of observation revive. Were it not for the apple-woman and the Armenian merchant and his dumb clerk, there is little in the London scenes to haunt the memory.

When Borrow treats of the publisher, of Francis Ardry, or of other town-dwellers, he is ill at ease, and his mind, to use a phrase of his own, is dry and unproductive. But place him in the grassy lane or by the gypsy encampment, and all this is changed. The thoughts arrive in their throngs, and he effaces himself as he listens to others. He has no righteous horror of thieves or cheats, because he feels that had his circumstances been similar he might have become as one of them. His mind is merely the medium through which the story flows upon his page ; it emerges as it left the lips of the teller, without colour from his personal idiosyncrasy : as the immortal discourse with Jasper Petulengro about the wind on the heath. Lavengro narrates the story of Peter Williams for its intrinsic worth, not for any enriching effect it has upon his own moral nature. His mind goes out to his characters, to those possessed by one idea which has made them wanderers on the face of the earth. And his treatment of nature is identical with that of man ; he does not seek nature, he is nature. Had he lived in the eighteenth century, as well he might, with what vigour would he have refuted Dr. Johnson's claim for the superiority of Fleet Street over the fairest sylvan scene. The modern dweller in towns is smitten with something of religious awe at meadows golden with buttercups or fruit trees in blossom. With Borrow they are man's rightful heritage, to be enjoyed, not worshipped. When Milton decks with flowers the bier of Lycidas, he reveals as much of his own mind as of their beauty ; but when Shakespeare's Perdita speaks of " daffodils that come before the swallow dares, and take the winds of March with beauty," it intoxicates us with the immortal hope of spring. Borrow wanders in nature's garden like one of its lawful possessors. The leafy canopy that shelters him from the sun, the cool stream to refresh his limbs, the tinkle of falling water, the light on grass : all these are not far removed like some

Promised Land, but ever present, and for lack of which man shall not grow old in health.

The episode of Isopel Berners is said to be no exception to the almost unnatural calm that broods over Borrow's pages. It is accepted as veracious, since Borrow never invented a character, and Professor Saintsbury, after remarking that there was an absence of passion in all his characters and that he was never in love, adds that he would not have made himself cut so poor a figure without cause. Mr. Seccombe affirms that Borrow's normal temper was a cold one, that he was a despiser and distruster of young women, and that he dallied with the project and insulted Isopel with his irony. Both these statements are too sweeping, though it may be conceded that Borrow spent the time with Isopel in the dingle somewhat strangely in teaching her Armenian. But to a man of his temperament, companionship and affectionate sympathy sufficed, as was proved by the happiness of his marriage to a woman older than himself who shared all his thoughts and copied his manuscripts for the printer. Actual love-making was alien to his nature, and he delighted in Isopel's presence in an unconscious manner. The Armenian lessons merely filled a gap in their conversations, as the sense in a certain kind of poetry is subordinate to the emotions expressed indirectly by the sound. Yet it may be doubted whether, since the serpent entered Eden, greater happiness has been vouchsafed to man than in this instance to Borrow.

Perhaps the strongest case for his detractors is the slightness of his regret for Isopel's departure, when every succeeding time the temptation to follow her grew more faint ; but we must remember that in him the man of action is always contending with the poet, and it is the nature of the man of action to live in the present and ever to seek new adventures. His books are composed of the imaginative aura that action gives off ; they are sagas in which he sings his own deeds. Although literal

records, they are touched with a retrospective enchant-
ment, as by one who has toiled all the morning, slept
at midday, and woken at sunset to find the prospect
unchanged yet transfigured. In the preface to *Lavengro*
he describes it as " a dream," and there is a passage in
the *Bible in Spain* telling of his joy in contemplating a
beautiful landscape, which throws an unconscious light
on the working of his genius : " An hour elapsed, and
I still maintained my seat on the wall ; the past scenes
of my life flitting before my eyes in airy and fantastic
array, through which every now and then peeped trees
and hills and other patches of the real landscape which
I was confronting——" Before the conclusion of
Romany Rye the glow had faded entirely from the
heavens, the real encroached more and more upon the
ideal. And the whole of *Wild Wales* was composed in
the light of common day.

Save for the single instance of the stage coachmen
and the coming of the railway, there is no reference to
contemporary life in Borrow's volumes of autobiography.
The stream waters the fields of childhood, enters the
green valley of youth chequered by the shadows of
domestic sorrow, and passes through the dark gorge of
London life. Then the hills fall back, the river spreads
into a lake on which the sunlight dances ; only our
charmed boat has no landmark by which to steer.
The *Bible in Spain* was held together by the state of the
country, the distribution of Testaments, the relations
of Borrow to the Spanish Government ; but for want
of such stiffening ideas the fabric of *Lavengro* is liable
to collapse upon the reader's mind.

Yet this unfettered simplicity is not all loss. We
may prove it by turning, after a study of Borrow, to the
works of any other writer of imaginative prose. At
once we are made aware of contracted horizons, of
having exchanged the boundless heath for the walks of
men, freedom for social tyranny. We visit other writers
at well-ordered times, and a guide escorts us along

gravel walks, and points out objects of interest. But the visitor to Borrow's domain must always find the lodge closed and the keeper gone. He is fortunate if, roaming round the immense circuit, he espies a little door unlatched ; but when he enters, what a wilderness meets his view ! And if one of the hilly and over-grown paths does lead him to the house-front, he discerns a long and rambling structure, in no single architectural style, but with the traces of every age upon its surface.

No discussion of Borrow's merits should omit some reference to his style. It is flexible but not emphatic ; it neither disturbs nor excites ; its epithets do not lance the reader's mind. It has a colloquial tinge, and does not disdain the set phrase ; we do not feel, as with some writers, of whom Milton is the grand exemplar, that every word has been re-dipped in the creative spring. But its rhythm is flawless, and pursues the reader as the long-drawn ebb of the sea pursues the traveller who turns his steps inland. It often wears a thin robe of irony, but when this is discarded, it less resembles thinking aloud than confession by letter or spoken word to an understanding friend. Take this from *Lavengro :* " When many years had rolled on, long after I had attained manhood, and had seen and suffered much, and when our first interview had long since been effaced from the mind of the man of peace, I visited him in his venerable hall, and partook of the hospitality of his hearth." Or this from the *Bible in Spain :* " In the streets of Aranjuez, and beneath the mighty cedars and gigantic elms and plantains which compose its noble woods, I have frequently seen groups assembled listening to individuals who, with the New Testament in their hands, were reading aloud the comfortable words of salvation." There is one book on which many writers have attempted to model their style, and of whose grand music we find some echoes in Borrow : " Oh, how dare I mention the dark feeling of mysterious dread which comes over the mind, and which the lamp of reason, though burning bright the while, is unable to dispel !——— In the brightest days of prosperity—in the midst of health and wealth—how sentient is the poor human creature of thy neighbourhood ! How instinctively aware that the flood-gates of horror may be cast open, and the dark stream engulf him for ever and ever ! "

Pater the Humanist

PATER THE HUMANIST

I

THERE was much talk at one time of a revival of poetry and the excellences of the Georgian poets. The spectator of the modern world, unpenetrated as it is by the spirit of beauty, cannot accept such cheering statements without question. The artistic nature demands enjoyment of life for its complete development ; indeed the plea advar ed by some poets for happiness has often seemed excessive ; yet there never was a time when the outer experience would accord less with the inward vision of beauty than the present. And to prove this we may select the instance of Pater, which, in so far as he was the typical artist, lies at the cross-roads of thought. Already he belongs to a past generation, yet he summarises the difficulties and triumphs of the artist beset by a utilitarian world.

It has been objected to Pater that what he sought was a state of mind rather than a motive for beneficent action, and the student of his life will hardly controvert this statement. Its very eventlessness was characteristic of him, as he himself remarked that the impersonality of Merimée's style was an effective personal trait. Like his own Marius, it was his custom " to take flight in time from any too disturbing passion." He declined marriage and the graver responsibilities ; and it is even recorded that he would at once leave a hotel in which any person spoke to him. He expended his imaginative affections upon the past, and retained a profound mistrust of the actual age in which he lived.

PATER THE HUMANIST

Pater stood for the humanities as opposed to the utilities and expediencies ; and in an age like the present his indeed would be a voice crying in the wilderness. The academic type of mind, of which he is the greatest example, is tending more and more to eclipse : and even the older universities are hardly withstanding the attacks of those who desire education to become practical. The pressure of competition is urging the adoption of business principles in every department of life ; indeed, the term " business " is becoming the fetish of the twentieth century, as " evolution " was of the later nineteenth. That such preoccupations defeat the ideal element in human nature is an obvious truth ; and as a result we see a universal sacrifice of beauty to the lust for gain, and an ever-increasing worship of Mammon.

It is well known that man's best nature appears in communion with but one other mind—as the sweetest of all human relationships testifies—that he is acted upon by the presence of numbers to less worthy self-expression. Some such transformation has been effected by the conditions of the modern world. Man's opportunities of retirement have become rarer, his anxieties external, and his hope of success or fear of loss limited to what is material. Agnostics of the type of Cotter Morison exulted in the downfall of orthodox belief, yet it is doubtful whether religion was such a fruitful source of terrors to the average man, and whether the imminence of hell was so unquestioned as they would have us believe. What the men of the seventeenth and eighteenth centuries did admit was the reality of conscience ; and this recognition of an invisible Overseer imparted to the character a dignity in which we who measure all actions according or not as they are approved by our fellow-men are lacking. The " religion of humanity " which was to cure all evils and herald the millennium, is looking sadly faded to the thoughtful mind : its message to the worldly man is, " Thou shalt not be found out."

PATER THE HUMANIST

The academic or disinterested type of mind like that of Pater is being fast submerged. One of the most gracious traditions of educated man, the judging of his fellow-creatures according to their individual powers, is being superseded by the standard of results alone. That men are either efficient or inefficient is the doctrine of the man of business,—and that scorn not tolerance should be meted to the inefficient. The chance of failure being more admirable than success has passed out of the sphere of practical life.

The artist has always tended to live with himself, but he fetched from the world the stuff of which his dreams are made, and never did one standing at his watch-tower gaze into such darkness as at the present. For this reason Pater sought inspiration from the past, among those ages where the outer life corresponded somewhat with the inner vision. But in him, as in all who live remote from the actual world, without sharing its duties, there is a certain unreality. His style is fundamentally sincere, and the emotions which he derives from the past are genuine, but they give light without warmth. Indeed, he often works in pure light rather than light and shade ; but the legendary and historical scenes which he restores to us lie as in the unaccustomed glow of a midnight sun.

After journeying through this land of the midnight sun, to which we may compare Pater's works, and pausing to review our impressions, we find them exceedingly complex. Pater was, above all, an artist, and, secondarily, critic, biographer, philosopher. The ultimate fact of his writings is an emotion, but the chain has been so surrounded by what seems acquired knowledge that a casual touch may not reveal it to be electric. In earlier days a purer form of literature might have suited Pater's genius, but a late civilization absorbs nearly all in criticism, and hence there is some want of balance between his form and content. This trait shows most in the autobiographical passages. His soul comes to us in intellectual semblance, as the Goddesses of his beloved Greek mythology veiled their beauty in the disguises of old women. Emotion is generated by the movement of the intellect—we must think in order to feel—and the meaning yields its sweetness in proportion as the reader's thought is intense. In the chapter of *Marius the Epicurean*, "The Will as Vision," it is revealed to Marius that he had never for one moment been left spiritually alone in the world, but an unfailing companion had always been by his side. We may regret that this singularly wistful idea was not disparted from some of its intellectual dress and preached in the outer courts of the Temple, where it might have increased Pater's disciples a thousandfold. Carlyle compared the *Iliad* to a star growing brighter as it grows more distant ; and if we watch the process of the mind in reading, shall we say, Fielding and Thackeray, who, often alike, belong to different ages, we see that with Fielding the emotion takes longer to reach us, as his star has receded further through time. Even so, Pater does not speak to us quite in our own language. The guest is gone before we discover that we have unawares entertained an angel.

II

The title *Imaginary Portraits*, which belongs to Pater's slenderest volume, might have included the greater portion of his critical work. Between him and his subject there is a deeper subconscious affinity than is usual with criticism. The reason is partly his own happy gift in selecting a kindred nature, for it is said he never wasted time in experimental reading,—and partly the period of brooding before composition which he exacted of himself. Indeed, he quotes with approval the ten years' meditation through which Sir Thomas Browne passed before writing *Urn Burial*. Hence, while seeming most impersonal, Pater is often the reverse, and, while apparently absorbed in his subject, he is unconsciously self-analytic. It is hard to write of him because he has himself made some of the best criticism on his own work. He tells us that Wordsworth's object was " impassioned contemplation " ; that Leonardo possessed the art " of tracking the sources of expression to their subtlest retreats " ; that Plato had " a sort of sensuous love of the unseen " ; that Botticelli " accepts that middle world in which men take no side in great conflicts, and decide no great issues, and make great refusals."

If, in writing of the ancient world, the balance is somewhat displaced, we owe to it Pater's most characteristic work. In *The Child in the House* he tells us how, parallel with his susceptibility to beauty, there grew up in him " an almost diseased sensibility to the spectacle of suffering," and, in the most beautiful chapter of *Marius,* how men are constructed for suffering, and feel sorrow in proportion to their moral or nervous perfection. He brings this capacity for sorrow to his survey of ancient times, and while seeming to contradict his former saying that the Greek lived a purely outer life, he interpolates into the myth of Demeter and Persephone that " worship of sorrow " which is said to be scrupulously modern. He defines romanticism as the desire for a beauty born of unlikely elements, and it is in his conception of the majestic figures of Demeter and Kore that he is romantic. He sees them either at sunrise or sunset, when they cast the longest shadows.

Similarly, who does not connect those tender scenes in the *Hippolytus* with Pater's self ? We have the " ancient twilight world " with its tradition of celestial visitants remote from the luxuries of Athens, and the mother who is shocked by " a sense of something unearthly in her boy's contentment," or relieved when it becomes " a shade less unconscious." Pater's affections were entwined with the church and the family, as the last institutions to preserve beauty in the modern world.

PATER THE HUMANIST

The habit of protracted meditation which has made of the greater part of Pater's work a kind of disguised autobiography, has left its print upon his style. Whether one can overdo even such an excellent habit as profound meditation before composition is a question that might with all diffidence be asked. It is true that we get his thought exactly transcribed, but is the thought still alive by the time it reaches the paper, after so long a sojourn in the chambers of his brain? Must the reader make too great an effort to reanimate it? A writer usually starts upon his subject with a certain number of ideas, and the struggle of the brain to co-ordinate these generates further ideas. We feel with Pater that he has waited till the process of generation is complete, and only when the descendants of the parent ideas have become infertile does he mark out the genealogical tree. At its worst an air of exhaustion hangs over his page, and nowhere is there the sudden delight of spontaneous generation from the chance meeting of wandering thoughts.

Although the separate parts have been previously completed in his mind and noiselessly joined together, so that the Temple rises to no sound of axe or hammer, the reader may test the solid foundation in his interest by his power to be strongly moved by certain phrases or even single words. Such is the term " narcotic " applied to the flowers most appropriately used at the worship of Demeter, or the often-repeated comparison to homesickness of man's thought of death.

The essayist was wont to greet us in our own language and speak of topics which we knew well as a means of winning our attention, but in the slow fire of Pater's long-choosing mind all earthly particles have perished, and he conducts us to the upper chamber of his thought not by the common stairway of sense. His message thus seems detached from experience, and the impression resembles that of a vivid dream.

And yet, considering the difficulties of the modern

writer working in an ancient material, this attitude of Pater's seems the only possible one. It was not only the Athenians who demanded some new thing, and a bore is best defined as one whose sayings may be foretold. When Candide arrived in the El Dorado country he picked up the gold that was lying by the roadside, and offered it for payment at an inn : which gold was returned to him with good-humoured laughter. Such treatment would be accorded now to the writer who dealt in the simple rhythms and emotions of the older poets. For even the greatest poetry falls less resonantly on the ears of a later generation ; it has become part of the common language, and as thousands speak it who have never consciously perused it, the shock of novelty is gone.

An intenser subjectivity, therefore, must distinguish a literature in its old age. In form and content it reflects the author's dread of besieging his reader's ears with a thrice-told tale. And one like Pater, in his anxiety of expending a single word that should draw the reader's attention from his own impression into the wider areas of settled thought, attenuates his meaning to a point that recalls the garment which could only be seen by the virtuous. Its imperceptible advance is the despair of the wandering mind. In glancing back it is almost impossible to say at what moment his message has been delivered, or which is the word that has converted us. The older writers, except in their most inspired moments, used words which a reader might transform according to his associations ; but the severer taste of modern times requires an author to abjure this language of the market-place. No word, or even portion of its meaning, must lie outside the radius of his personality. Hard beset in his efforts to mark out new areas from chaos with his golden compasses, he finds in his own soul the one new thing.

The simplicity of a style like this is not what we usually understand by the word. It is that of age rather than youth ; not of one who knows little of books, but who has read deeply and consciously refrains from expressing his thought in terms that recall men's accumulated wisdom. As an instance we may cite that passage in *Gaston de Latour* describing Montaigne's relations with the friend of his life : " Yet, after all, were he pressed to say why he had so loved Étienne de la Boétie, he could but answer : ' Because it was He ! Because it was I ! ' "

Charlotte Brontë

CHARLOTTE BRONTË

WHEN the stir of thought caused by the publication in *The Times*[1] of Charlotte Brontë's four letters to Professor Heger has subsided, it will be found that they do not add substantially to our knowledge of one whose self-expression in her books was entire. They furnish, it is true, biographical facts, and they reveal the extent of the Professor's irresponsiveness ; but the task of the psychological critic of the future will be, as in the past, to define the exact nature of Charlotte Brontë's spiritual emotion. And in all probability we shall find the truth somewhere between the opinions formerly advanced by Mr. Clement Shorter and Mr. Angus MacKay ; always bearing in mind, when making our estimate, Charlotte Brontë's intense craving for human sympathy, and the cruelty of circumstance which compelled the waste of her faculty for friendship. Mr. MacKay, without attempting to cast the slightest aspersion on her character, maintained that she was smitten with a veritable passion, and laid stress on the predominance of the love agony in her pages, of the theme of unrequited affection, of the frequency of love scenes between master and pupil, of Heger's appearance under different forms in all her books. He was the first man of intellectual gifts with whom she had associated, and " the ripening of friendship and gratitude into a stronger feeling would be by imperceptible stages, and she herself would not know

[1] July, 1913.

147

when that line was crossed. . . ." In this sense Mr. MacKay interpreted the passage in Charlotte Brontë's letter that she returned to Brussels against her conscience and was punished by the withdrawal for two years of happiness and peace of mind ; and the further statement : " I think, however long I live, I shall not forget what the parting with M. Heger cost me." Against this we have Mr. Shorter's warning that it is " an act of treachery to a great writer's memory to attempt to pry too closely into his heart." In his opinion, Charlotte Brontë kept all such thoughts well in subjection ; only, perhaps, when in a neurotic state she " permitted herself to think of the might-have-beens of life."

There is at least no doubt that Charlotte Brontë's sojourn at Brussels was the intellectual turning-point of her life, and that had it not been for Heger's mental drilling, it is doubtful whether her subsequent writings would have taken the shape they did. She had, during childhood and girlhood, covered reams of paper with her tiny writing, but not one of these stories now possesses independent interest. Miss Frederika Macdonald has told us that it was Heger who first persuaded Charlotte Brontë that art was necessary to carry conviction to the reader ; that the man of genius does not produce without labour ; and that genius without art is like force without the lever.

It may therefore be asserted that Brussels was the intellectual stimulus of Charlotte Brontë's creative faculty, and partially the moral one ; and more than this it is not permissible to add. For a study of her writings convinces that the melancholy impression they leave is not from unrequited affection, but from the circumstances which made it imperative for their heroines to win love. And here we touch the autobiographical roof-tree of Charlotte Brontë's house of fame. It is the disharmonies of her life—passion and hypochondria, love of sociality and enforced solitude.

One of Charlotte Brontë's characteristics most strongly

emphasized by Mrs. Gaskell is her constitutional absence of hope, and we see in *Villette* how insistently the heroine confesses to this trait. Of course, the roll of tragedies in her life was a heavy one. It began in 1825, when she was nine years old, with the deaths of her elder sisters Maria and Elizabeth, and concluded in 1848–9, when the events of a few months were the death of her disgraced brother Branwell, and the deaths from consumption of her remaining sisters, Emily and Anne. And yet there were causes other than external which forbade happiness to Charlotte Brontë. Her malady of hypochondria was as much physical as mental. " My art halts at the threshold of hypochondria," says Dr. John in *Villette* ; " she just looks in and sees a chamber of torture, but can neither say nor do much. Cheerful society would be of use——" But perhaps the fullest exposition is that of Crimsworth in the *Professor* :—

" She (Hypochondria) had been my acquaintance, nay, my guest, once before in boyhood ; I had entertained her at bed and board for a year ; for that space of time I had her to myself in secret ; she lay with me, she ate with me, she walked out with me, showing me nooks in woods, hollows in hills, where we could sit together, and where she could drop her drear veil over me and so hide sky and sun, grass and green tree ; taking me entirely to her death-cold bosom, and holding me with arms of bone. What tales she would tell me at such hours ! What songs she would recite in my ears ! How she would discourse to me of her own country—the grave—and again and again promise to conduct me there ere long ; and, drawing me to the very brink of a black, sullen river, show me, on the other side, shores unequal with mound, monument, and tablet, standing up in a glimmer more hoary than moonlight. ' Necropolis ! ' she would whisper, pointing to the pale piles, and add, ' It contains a mansion prepared for you.' "

The cheerful society which Dr. John prescribed for Lucy Snowe was too often withheld from Charlotte Brontë. We see this dependence upon surroundings in the heroines of her books and in herself ; how, when outer impressions became less acute, the mind preyed upon itself. When she returned to Brussels, her friend Mary Taylor tells us that now that " she had become acquainted with the people and ways her life became monotonous, and she fell into the same hopeless state as at Miss Wooler's." The author of a recent critical work has censured Byron because he was first a man and then a poet, because the external world was more real to him than the internal. It is this disharmony between the two worlds that made the tragedy of Charlotte Brontë's life and gave to her writings their note of piercing regret. And at last, when a chance of happiness did offer itself, she scarcely dared step forward and secure it. She yielded to her father's objections to her marriage because her unhoping nature, to which circumstances had given tragic corroboration, made her a timid loiterer on the shore of the sea of life.

Turning to her writings, we will speak first of the *Professor*, which, in spite of its many rejections and tardy birth, is a book that still gives pleasure to read, independent of its mighty successors. It sounds no great depth of human character, and is not fervid with passion ; but it is not exclusively the chrysalis whence emerged in later years the brilliant butterfly of *Villette*. Except passion, we have all the constituents of the style that subsequently underwent development rather than change ; but the faults of construction, never entirely eliminated, are at their worst. The interest is well sustained because of the writer's sincerity, but threads are dropped and resumed at random, contrasts, as between Crimsworth and his brutal brother, are too glaring, and the episodes are out of proportion. The surroundings of X—— (Huddersfield) and Crimsworth Hall are so admirably depicted that we are loth to part with them for good in the course of a few pages ; and although incidents succeed without pause, they do not at once dissipate the regrets in the reader's mind. The theme is one that Charlotte Brontë was afterwards to treat with greater power : that of an individual without friends or fortune who must fight his way to happiness through a hostile world. But the interest centres less in individual character than in the contrast of the Belgian type with the English, and the observation of Belgian school life through English eyes. It is the writer's conviction of the truth of this observation that gives the book its permanent value.

Both French and Belgian character are treated from the insular point of view. The cry of the exile and the heretic rings throughout the book. No greater tribute can be paid to any custom than to say it recalls something English. When Crimsworth and Pelet take coffee together, the comfort is " almost English." It is the English accent of Frances Henri that first thrills Crimsworth's heart. Part of his love is the satisfaction in her presence of the exile's yearning.

In *Jane Eyre* the quality of passion appears. In the *Professor* the words returned no echoes, the interval between the striking of the notes was not filled by the pedal-music of passion. There was the same difference as between the classical school of Pope and the romantic school of Wordsworth. In one the object is seen clearly against a clean sky ; in the other it is transfigured by haze or cloud or distance. In the first there is beauty ; in the second, beauty and strangeness.

This quality of strangeness springs from the union of passion and imagination, which transfigure the ordinary scenes of life, and we listen to her in gathering awe as to the traveller from whose lips fall tidings of unknown lands. In a book such as the *Pilgrim's Progress* our fear is of the burning pit ; in the *Faerie Queene* of dragons and enchanters ; but in *Jane Eyre* it is of something vague and unformed. It differs from the earlier books as the terrors of the Puritan of the seventeenth century differed from those of the believing-agnostic of the nineteenth, as *Grace Abounding* differed from *Sartor Resartus*. The power in its essence is that of the mind to transmute by means of emotion, to modify external scenes according to the joy or sorrow of which they have been the witnesses ; and it is effective in proportion as memory or the subconscious self in sleep or dreams tinge the pictures of the past with deeper shades. Even the child who reads the *Pilgrim's Progress* finds such objects as the wicket-gate, the foot-path, the stile between two fields, transfigured by the writer's spiritual fervour. And for this reason the industry which has identified all the places mentioned in the Brontë novels with their originals is, from the literary point of view, misplaced. In reading *Jane Eyre* we cannot help feeling mildly surprised when a chance allusion reminds us that the scene is laid in a northern or north-midland county, or even in England at all. Our state of mind is inverse to that of the individual who read *Gulliver's Travels* and looked for Lilliput on the map. We should recall a pregnant sentence in an *Athenæum*[1] article on Charlotte Brontë : " Crises and partings, journeys and reunions, in her pages sometimes seem to tell of people in more mysterious lands and on more mysterious seas than ours. They speak of souls rather than of bodies."

Charlotte Brontë is more akin to the poets of the romantic revival than to the other leading English novelists, all of whom have one thing in common that she has not. They are profoundly concerned with the things of this world ; while with her we feel that the earth is but one point with an " unfathomed gulf " on each side, that all the rest is " formless cloud and vacant depth," and we shudder " at the thought of tottering and plunging amid that chaos." A book like *Jane Eyre* belongs to no epoch or state of society ; it is simply a story told by a lonely human being. The action of Fielding, of Scott, of Miss Austen, of George Eliot, takes place on the sunlit plain ; with Charlotte Brontë it is fought out on inaccessible mountains, among sharp peaks, or in deep valleys where the shadows lie thickest.

[1] April 7th, 1900.

The causes of this must be sought in those conditions of Charlotte Brontë's life which combined to render her morbid. For she was not by nature austere ; she had a passionate craving for companionship and for love, and a passionate apprehension of the beauty of the world. Her love of colour is seen not only in her descriptions of nature—in moonlit skies and blossoming orchards— but in details such as dress fabrics and the decorations of a room. But she was condemned, even before the death of her sisters, to much suffering and solitude, as in her governess days and the fateful second year at Brussels. She sought the consolations of love, because these alone could absorb her mind and interpose between it and the empty horizons of life—as some persons turn to an unreasoned faith from the horrors of scepticism. It is the morbidity that springs from solitary brooding, from the constitutional absence of hope that Mrs. Gaskell noted, and from lowness of vitality, that casts those strange shadows over the landscape of her novels. The feeling may be communicated by a simple descriptive touch, as when Jane Eyre at twilight turns with a shudder from the closet where her " wraith-like " wedding apparel hangs ; but more usually by the aspects of nature. Charlotte Brontë's kinship to the poets is no- where more unquestioned than in her treatment of nature. To say that nature forms the background of the action is to understate the case. Nature grieves or rejoices with the actors, warns of coming danger, blends with their minds and reflects their emotions. And the scent of flowers, the loneliness of a road, the desolation of the moors, the changes of the seasons or of night and day, the tinkle of streams that thread remote hill-passes, heard in the quiet of evening—seem to suggest how slender a foothold has man on life and happiness, and how great the mystery that lies beyond. Small wonder that Rochester tells Jane Eyre she has the look of another world on her face.

It is the disharmony of her life, as it was and as it

might have been, that forms the persistent motive in Charlotte Brontë's novels. How often do we find a repetition in the spirit of that scene early in the *Professor* where Crimsworth, grudgingly admitted to his brother's house, casts yearning glances at the group of girls " enveloped in silvery clouds of white gauze and muslin," and feels himself isolated and ignored. These feelings of injustice and exclusion must have been Charlotte Brontë's when, as governess, she had experience of " the dark side of ' respectable ' human nature." " A complaint to the mother only brings black looks on myself," she wrote ; and, " I find it so hard to repel the rude familiarity of children." Her inability to deal with children is not surprising when we recall her own motherless childhood, and the serious pursuits that took the place of games at Haworth Parsonage.

The charge of faulty construction is frequently brought against Charlotte Brontë's novels ; indeed, the least critical reader must suffer at times from having his interest in old scenes violently uprooted and transferred. If something is conceded to the requirements of autobiography, the residue can only be explained as the defects of Charlotte Brontë's qualities. The difficulties of the literary artist, like those of the orator, are not in linking one subject to another, but in keeping the whole before his readers or audience, so that the entire weight of the argument presses on their minds. In *David Copperfield*, Dickens, though flitting from scene to scene, keeps his communications open, because his action takes place on the broad earth, unlike the spiritual heights of Charlotte Brontë. With her, each winding of the valley is shut off by a wall of rock. No sooner does the heroine quit her surroundings than they are swallowed up in darkness. The episodes are successive catastrophes whence she alone escapes to tell the tale. It is the predominance of soul-history that causes this periodical quenching of the interest : the abrupt dismissal from the circle of the narrative of those whose work in stimulating the emotions of the central figure is done. We can well believe that Lowood stood in a hollow girdled by hills like barriers of separation between it and the living world. That Mr. Rochester should have heard independently of Mr. Brocklehurst, that Jane Eyre while at Thornfield should revisit Gateshead, come with a shock of surprise. That roads should exist and communications pass between such places, strains our credulity as much as the second part of the *Pilgrim's Progress* when Christiana follows in her husband's steps through the dread country.

The second scene of the book takes place at Lowood Orphan Asylum, subsequently identified with Cowan Bridge. All Charlotte Brontë's best work had a basis of reality, and perhaps she never wrote anything more poignant than the description of Lowood and the character of Helen Burns. In homely but graphic words she speaks of physical hardships and privations ; not the least distressing of her pictures is that of the pale thin girls herded in the garden verandah, during the hour of recreation, where the sound of a hollow cough was not infrequent. The prototype of Helen Burns was Maria Brontë, whose beautiful mind was mated with untidy habits ; and these made her the victim of the pitiless Miss Scatcherd. The shock of witnessing the indignities meted to her idolized sister permanently affected Charlotte Brontë's mental health, and explains the freshness of indignation with which the lines of the picture are wrought after twenty-five years of suppressed but passionate brooding. It is in the death of Helen Burns from consumption that the feeling of strangeness is most accentuated ; when Jane Eyre, returning at sunset from wandering in the woods, enquires after her friend, and receiving the answer, " She will not be here long," seeks the sick chamber through the rambling old house by moonlight.

The central episode of *Jane Eyre* is Thornfield, and here Charlotte Brontë abandoned her resolve never to affect " one feeling on any subject that I do not really experience." Some of the less essential matter was reproduced from her own life ; the following passage in one of her letters expresses feelings akin to those of Jane among Mr. Rochester's guests : " The only glimpses of society I have ever had were obtained in my vocation as governess, and some of the most miserable moments I can recall were passed in drawing-rooms full of strange faces." But the truth of the autobiography lies in its inwardness ; as Jane Eyre says to Mr. Rochester : " It is my spirit that addresses your spirit." Many as are the indictments of Rochester, we cannot condemn one who is responsible for the rise of such an Aladdin's palace of joy in a lonely heart. Also, the characters of the book are developed in proportion as they affect the heroine's inner life, and every event moves us according as it advances or retards the happiness for which she craves. When, towards the close, we hear of the burning of Thornfield, we tremble till we know that Rochester has escaped, but it is less for his own sake than for Jane's.

Shirley is the table-land between the peaks of *Jane Eyre* and *Villette*. It is founded on observation and hearsay rather than inner experience ; only at times, as we traverse its broad spaces, do we light upon autobiographical rock. The action takes place in 1811–12, the years of the Luddite riots, stories of which had been told to Charlotte Brontë as a child by her father, who had first-hand acquaintance with some of the events, and by her schoolmistress, Miss Wooler. But Charlotte Brontë leavened the historical characters with many of her own generation. And *Shirley* may be described as her most social book because the interest is diffused among a score of persons, not centred in one. Among the more favoured of these it is Charlotte Brontë who was beloved by her schoolfellows at Roe Head, who spent week-ends with her friends, Ellen Nussey and Mary Taylor, and in the house of the latter took part in fiery political discussions, opposing her Tory immobility to Radical onsets. With the less favoured, it is Charlotte Brontë, the somewhat sententious little clergyman's daughter. In any case, *Shirley* is her most persistent attempt at a novel of manners, and to bring into artistic focus characters of independent interests.

There are structural faults in *Shirley;* the groups of characters lack fusion, and are not tributaries of one main narrative stream. The action is slow-moving, incident arises chiefly from the shocks of antagonistic characters. And, despite the extraordinary vividness with which these characters start up on her pages, they hardly satisfy the requirements of a novel of manners in being typical. But these are defects of Charlotte Brontë's qualities. She had, as Swinburne said, " the very rarest of all powers or faculties of imagination applied to actual life and individual character." Like her sister Anne, she transcribed what was before her eyes, but the methods of the two differed as photography from portrait-painting. The first reproduces reality in the light of common day : the second links its subjects, with all their personal idiosyncrasies, to the ideas of which they are the symbols, and so discovers a path into the infinite. Anne had neither the imagination nor the powerful intellect capable of brooding intensely over the real till it was transfigured into the ideal. And yet Charlotte Brontë did not divine how literal were her renderings of nature ; she once wrote to Ellen Nussey that she only suffered reality to " suggest," never to " dictate." Circumstances confuted her theory, for the publication of *Shirley* marked the term of her anonymity as a writer.

Yet, with all their vividness, the figures in *Shirley* are seen rather in low relief than rounded completeness. For Charlotte Brontë lacked that higher kind of humour which can view shocks of temperament with an indulgent if melancholy smile. She saw matter for tears rather than smiles in the seeming-small imperfections by which

happiness is just missed both for self and others, and
at those sharp angles of character which intercept the
sunlight from neighbouring spirits. And her method
of satirising the foibles she deemed most harmful proved
her range of sympathies to be but narrow. The words
" subjective " and " objective " have fallen into ill
repute, yet they do contain a meaning expressed by no
others. All classification is arbitrary, but there does
exist a point, below which when the mind narrows, and
above which when it broadens, communications may
not pass. And Charlotte Brontë's place is on the subjective side.

In Xenophon's *Memorabilia* Socrates observes that
human beings must tolerate each other's faults because
they require each other ; and this was precisely in-
applicable to Charlotte Brontë. With strong leanings
towards sociality, she had been condemned to live in
isolation till her habits grew fixed and she became
independent and fastidious. " For society, long seclusion
has in a great measure unfitted me," she once wrote to
Mr. W. S. Williams ; " I doubt whether I should
enjoy it if I might have it. Sometimes I think I should,
and I thirst for it ; but at other times I doubt my cap-
ability of pleasing or deriving pleasure. The prisoner
in solitary confinement, the toad in the block of marble,
all in time shape themselves to their lot." Hence there
is a certain unkindness in her satire, there is " the
keenness of home criticism " directed against a world
she viewed with the detachment of a spectator. She
has also the spirit of reprisal ; she hits back because
she has been hit. The shortcomings on which she lays
her finger are those which must have jarred the sensitiveness of the recluse who at rare intervals ventures into the
world. When she speaks of Mr. Donne's harsh voice
and vulgarly presumptuous and familiar style, we can
well believe it was that voice and that style which had
thrown her nerves into an agony ; it would have pleased
her to think that he had read the passage and winced

at the allusion. How great is the gulf between the equanimity of Miss Austen, or the wide-embracing tolerance of George Eliot, who shows how the limitations of humble intellects recoil as much upon themselves as upon the susceptibilities of others.

The action of the book moves slowly as one group or another hold the stage. Now we are with Shirley under the oak beams of Fieldhead, now with the Yorkes at Briarmains, now at the Rectory or Hollows Cottage ; anon the curates are called in to make sport for us. But the two central characters are Caroline Helstone and Shirley Keeldar ; and if one can say that the interest of the book is ever brought to a focus, it is in their love for the brothers Moore. Caroline has some kinship with the heroines of Byron's romances, the Zuleikas and Medoras, in whom passive natures and mild manners co-exist with power to love greatly. She is believed to be a composition of Ellen Nussey and Anne Brontë, but the mind is that of Charlotte herself. We do not feel the immense solitudes that surround Jane Eyre and Lucy Snowe ; it is rather the social side of Charlotte that is revealed. No doubt the charming externals are borrowed from Ellen and Anne, and also such qualities of temperament as sensitiveness to the moods of others, and renunciation without a struggle. But when the deeps of character are laid bare it is Charlotte Brontë herself. Yet Anne also was at times subject to religious melancholy, and we are reminded of both sisters when phrases escape from Caroline such as, " Every path trod by human feet terminates in one bourne—the grave," or " The soul's real hereafter, who shall guess ? "

Shirley herself was admitted by Charlotte Brontë to be a representation of Emily's lighter side. Except her love of animals, there is little in Shirley to recall anything we know of Emily, and in her social leanings there is one strange anachronism. There is truth in the criticism that Caroline was the child of nature and Shirley the creature of circumstance. To Shirley's position of heiress is due some portion of her charm ; to the simplicity of character, the wistfulness and nonchalance that she preserves amid riches, to her forlorn bearing when surrounded by her worldly relations. And interest is heightened in her by a number of external touches. Compared with the " snow-white dove " of Caroline, she is the " gem-tinted bird of paradise." She is interesting by her purple silk dress and embroidered scarf, and by the daintiness of her appurtenances—the small satin bag, the clean, delicate glove—that the adoring Louis Moore finds scattered about her desk.

Such are the impressions left by a saunter through the long gallery of *Shirley*, and a survey of the portraits as they hang in the strongly marked light and shade of the author's predilections. And if their eyes haunt us long after we have turned away, it is because they were limned by no hasty hand. When Helstone or Yorke to name no others—are first introduced, we feel at once how intimately known to the author they are,—because their intense individuality is the outcome of years of mental attrition. And *Shirley* was Charlotte Brontë's most social book ; there is a joyousness in it which, although not persistent, breaks out at intervals through the whole, despite the triple catastrophe that suspended its making. Over the favoured characters is shed something of the charm of an age that has passed away. The Briarfield that Charlotte Brontë knew was already submerged by the manufacturing tide, but in her pages Fieldhead stands amid green fields, and Hollows Mill is the one blot on the unblackened country. There is Nunnely Common " pearled with daisies and golden with kingcups," and Nunnwood, " the sole remnant of antique British forest." A ramble through the *Shirley* country would be of endless profit to the Brontë enthusiast. The reverse of this was said about *Jane Eyre ;* and although *Villette* is in part a novel of manners, at any moment mists may roll down the mountains to blot out the villages at their base and make us wanderers in the strange country of the soul.

Three years intervened between the publication of *Shirley* and *Vilette* ; they were the bitterest of Charlotte Brontë's life. Death had been busy in her circle, and had justified her constitutional absence of hope. " I have seen her turn pale and feel faint," said one of her friends in former days, " when in Hartshead Church someone accidentally remarked that we were walking over graves. Charlotte was certainly afraid of death, not only of dead bodies or dying people. She dreaded it as something horrible." That not only Charlotte but Emily and Anne also were preoccupied with the physical aspects of death, abundant allusions in their novels and poems testify. Perhaps the situation of Haworth Parsonage and their familiarity from childhood with the facts of mortality account for the churchyard taint in their writings. But if this impersonal dread was present to Charlotte in happier days, how was it now when thrice within a few months she had seen " a marble calm succeed the last dread agony ? " What her life was during those years we may see from her letters ; how she sat in a lonely room with the clock ticking loud through a still house, and thought of the three laid in their narrow dark dwellings ; how the arrival of the post was her one link with the world, but when day after day brought nothing, her spirits fell so low that she was shocked at her dependence on it ; how the exercise of imagination alone afforded her pleasure, but " even imagination will not dispense with the ray of domestic cheerfulness." The visits she paid to London tended but slightly to mitigate her lot. Habit had unfitted her to enter the social territories conquered by her genius, and the physical pains produced by shyness were unabated. True happiness existed for her only in the brief visits of her friend Ellen. When at her worst, in the winter of 1851–2, she found it needful to anticipate a visit which she had conscientiously postponed till the work, eagerly desired by her publishers, was in their hands. " Let me see your dear face just for one reviving week," she wrote ; and when this week was over, her next letter concludes : " I do miss my dear companion. No more of that calm sleep." Hence there is a note of sharper anguish in *Villette ;* the shadow of a bereaved home falls on every page. We have travelled far from the sociality of *Shirley ;* we have returned, with fuller experience, to the bleakness of *Jane Eyre.* And over the new territories of her soul that Charlotte Brontë opens to our view is shed something of the pallor of a lunar landscape.

We have only to read the first pages of *Villette* to realize that it springs from a mind surcharged with sorrow. Hazlitt likened the effect of Dante's poetry to that produced by gazing on the face of one who had seen an object of horror ; and so we feel that the author of *Villette* has watched in the death-chamber and heard by the graveside the rattle of earth on coffins. She sits at her desk with the numbed senses of one restored to a world whence all she loves has been taken, and discovers what an immeasurable distance the tide of life has receded. Of Jane Eyre it may be said that we know every stripe the world has laid upon her from her birth ; but she is passing through a novitiate of suffering, while her elder sister, Lucy Snowe, has taken the black veil. In her heart there are reservoirs of tears wept before the first chapter of *Villette* was written. Jane Eyre had all to win of fate, but from Lucy Snowe fate had taken even what she had. She is now convinced that " fate is her permanent foe," and resolved to be a mere looker-on at life. But although the opening chapters treat of the pains of others, it is less for these that we feel than for her who interprets them with so much authority. The interest is in the author's personality, and it leads us like a pillar of cloud and fire across great wastes.

The constructional faults of the earlier books are reduced to a minimum. The episodic nature of *Jane Eyre* exacted that at intervals we should be detained among shallows ; in *Villette* a strong flood tide seizes us at the outset and bears us on till we descry a shore, if haply an elusive one. Twice indeed the scene is shifted before we reach Villette itself, but there is not the fullness of detail to delude us into believing each time that here is our abiding place. The fairy child Paulina is seen as in a long perspective ; her grief at separation from her father is less heart-piercing for its own sake than for the capacity for suffering which it reveals and will be hers with tenfold increase when a woman. Later on we contemplate " the steam-dimmed lattice " of Miss Marchmont's sick chamber ; and her sad memories move us less in themselves than for the understanding heart of her quiet companion. And yet, despite the absorbing autobiographical interest, the characters in *Villette* are presented with greater completeness. Mrs. Bretton, Dr. John, Ginevra Fanshawe are not in low relief like those of *Shirley ;* all their sides are turned to the world. The author judges them less by her own preferences and aversions than as workers under the eye of the taskmaster Fate, who to her had been so cruel. Even a fleeting vision of the king of Labassecour wakes her pity, because she discerns in the lines of his countenance traces of her own malady of hypochondria.

The opening scenes reflect a mind which feels by proxy ; with the transference of the action to the town of Villette (Brussels), the story proper begins. Belgian school life had already been treated in the *Professor*, and much of that then unpublished book was here reproduced. Many of the portraits, notably that of Madame Beck, were skilfully elaborated ; but the spirit of the whole is unchanged. There is the same anti-Catholic prejudice, the revolt against the subtle and all-pervading essence of Romanism, the feeling of exile in a land of convents and confessionals, the presence of a bar between her mind and those that were being reared in slavery. How far the delineations of character are historically true is beyond our scope ; the literary critic must be content with the imaginative truth which he finds in abundance.

The English group are considered by Lucy Snowe largely according to the contrast their lives offer with her own, and not without something of the pity that the poet Gray lavished upon the " little victims " in the Eton playing fields ; or as one treading a sombre avenue might behold at the far end a band of children gambolling in shafts of sunlight. She is angry with Ginevra Fanshawe because the best things in life come to her unsought, and she squanders them through want of appreciation. Her visits to the Brettons are like glimpses of home ; she notes every domestic detail with the eyes of one to whom such things are strange ; and not without apprehension that this pleasant, sheltered household is yet subject to chance and death and mutability.

Although the action of *Villette* takes place in a town, there is no diminution of the poetical quality which allies nature with the moods of the soul. Nature with Charlotte Brontë always symbolized the passing of time and the nearness of the grave. In the " forbidden alley " of the garden stood an old pear-tree " dead all but a few boughs which still faithfully renewed their perfumed snow in spring and their honey-sweet pendants in autumn." And again : " All the long, hot summer day burned away like a Yule log ; the crimson of its close perished ; I was left bent among the cool blue shades, over the pale and ashen gleams of its night." Like the iron mountain in the Arabian tale, she draws everything to herself, so that solid terrestrial objects are shaped to the bidding of her mind. She weaves the spell of loneliness round the school ; it is a " demi-convent secluded in the built-up core of a capital " ; the class-rooms are " great dreary jails buried far back beyond thoroughfares." The interest of the episodes, even when most impersonal, is measured by the ebb and flow of the writer's spiritual excitation. This quality is in abeyance so long as the external world maintains its power ; as during her first months in the Rue Fossette while she is occupied in observing and taking her bearings ; or on her visits to the Brettons. But it is ever ready to burst forth when the internal river of melancholy is in flood, as in the wonderful account of the visit to the confessional.

Friendship with the Brettons imparts to her life a human interest. Till then she had been content with the negation of suffering, convinced that fate was her permanent foe. She compared herself to an unobtrusive article of furniture, not striking enough to interest, not prominent enough to offend ; descriptions such as " quiet Lucy Snowe," " inoffensive shadow," did not distress her. She was a mere looker-on at life ; only, as she says, " when I thought of past days, I *could* feel." When Dr. John fulfils his promise of corresponding, she can scarce credit her good fortune. Attracted by the brilliant Paulina, he insensibly passes from the stage ; less godlike than Lucy once thought, but always to be remembered kindly.

The pang of separation is less sharp because of the striking figure that steps into the vacant place. Professor Paul Emanuel, the best loved and most vividly presented of all Charlotte Brontë's creations, is, to use a phrase of her own, " daguerreotyped by a pencil of keen lightning." He is the " waspish little despot " who " fumes like a bottled storm " ; so hasty in his movements that the folding doors " split " rather than open to his touch ; he makes crusades against the *amour propre* of all but himself ; he flees the presence of those he cannot outshine ; he hates intellectual supremacy in women, and " his veins were dark with a livid bella-donna tincture, the essence of jealousy." The sudden shifting of heroes has been made the ground of detrimental criticism, yet there is much to be said for the effects of contrast and surprise. And perhaps those of us who first became acquainted with *Villette* in early uncritical days will never forget our feelings of wonder and delight as we realized that the irascible little professor was softening into a lover.

Of M. Paul it was said by Leslie Stephen[1] : " We see only his relations to the little scholastic circle, and have no such perception as the greatest writers would give us of his relations to the universe, or, as the next order would give, of his relations to the great world without." May we not answer that *Villette* is in essentials an autobiography, and that M. Paul is less admirable as an independent specimen of humanity than as one who promotes the growth of its author's soul ? Apart from the effect of the heroine, the author's triumph is in having established the relativity of M. Paul's characteristics, so that he impresses the reader as entirely lovable, and his faults pass like clouds from the surface of the deep well of tenderness in his central nature.

The craving for companionship and love, the motive of *Jane Eyre*, and of Charlotte Brontë's life, is that of *Villette* ; but the world which is new to Jane Eyre is old to Lucy Snowe. Hardly, unwillingly, is she drawn into the pursuit ; only, being human, even she cannot escape the universal destiny while she inhabits what Teufelsdröckh called the " Place of Hope." The passion is a deeper one than Jane Eyre's for Rochester, because the need is greater ; into a greater loneliness must she relapse if unsuccessful. The question whether M. Paul ever returned from the exile to which " a woman's envy and a priest's bigotry " consigned him, is unsolved. Probably most conscientious readers, after many attempts at self-deception, will agree that the ship which bore him made one of the wrecks which strewed the Atlantic. Hopelessness is the prevailing note of the book in which Charlotte Brontë's powers culminated ; no other lies in such a depth of shadow as *Villette*.

That Charlotte Brontë suffered much during her solitary year at Brussels is obvious to every student of her life ; but when she wrote *Villette* in later Haworth days,

[1] *Hours in a Library*, Vol. III.

amid solitude and ill-health following bereavements, her memories of the Pensionnat Heger had been subjected to the idealizing process of time, and she must have recurred with peculiar fondness to days when she did fill some place in the living world, however unsympathetic were all but one of the figures which peopled it, when she had allotted tasks and duties as bulwarks between herself and the great ocean of melancholy. Much of *Villette* is a transcript from life, much of it is allegory. When M. Paul sailed away from Lucy Snowe, his prow was turned towards another shore than Guadeloupe ; and as we close the book there recur to us those penetrating words of the *Athenæum* reviewer : " Crises and partings, journeys and reunions in her pages sometimes seem to tell of people in more mysterious lands and on more mysterious seas than ours. They speak of souls rather than of bodies."

Edward Fitzgerald and his Times

EDWARD FITZGERALD AND HIS TIMES

A FEW hundred lines of inspired verse, and four volumes of correspondence possessing a distinctive charm, are what remain of FitzGerald's passage through the world. It is no longer the fashion to bewail scanty production, or we might ask why from a life which covered all but a few years of the nineteenth century, and to which abundant leisure was vouchsafed, more copious streams did not flow. Suffice it that what we have is of his best, and that the causes of his limited output are not without interest.

FitzGerald fell upon an age profoundly unsuited to his genius. One virtue of the poet he had to its full, the virtue of simplicity ; and he lived at a time when the evils of industrialism and commercialism were destroying man's primitive nature. In literature he loved the simple authors, such as Shakespeare, Cervantes, Boccaccio, Scott, for their broad human delight ; and he no less affected the simple joys of life. The friendships of his youth would have sufficed him for happiness in old age, had not the striving century been inimical to the preservation of such ties. It is not needful for a man to play a leading part among his fellows in order to reflect the spirit of the age. As Carlyle says : " The great world-revolutions send in their disturbing billows to the remotest creek."

The changes which had begun to transform the country about half a century before FitzGerald's birth were operating upon the hearts of men. We are grown so

used to an industrial England as scarcely to realize
that, historically speaking, it is of recent date ; that
what we know as the modern world came into being in
the reign of George III. The changes between 1750
and 1800 have been called revolution ; those between
1800 and 1900, although more far-reaching, less revolution than development. The town ever tended to grow,
and the fresh country withered at its touch. Village
industries were abandoned, and hard upon each other
came the spinning-jenny, the power-loom, the foundry,
the railway and canal. In 1801 the census returns
for England and Wales were under nine million ; a
hundred years later they were thirty-two and a half
million. And with this increased population came a
severer struggle to exist.

The crowding of men in cities, with facilities of inter-
communication, has done much to destroy the feeling
of the mystery of life. The poetic, like the religious
soul, faints for want of solitude and communion with
nature. The poet, like Wordsworth, may seek wild
and remote scenes, but nowadays we ask ourselves in
vain what place is wild and remote ? What place is
undisturbed by the railway, and the daily newspaper with
its hated murmurings of town life ? In former centuries,
when England was still a " sylvan wilderness," when
villages lived their little lives untouched by the world
beyond, when the few who travelled did so by stage
coach,—the soul of man still had glimpses of the immortal sea. Stevenson tells how the settlers on the empty
plains of Nebraska are afflicted by a " sickness of vision."
They are " tortured by the distance," and their eyes
" quail before so vast an outlook." A reverse process
takes place in the town-dweller of to-day. His interests
are crowded into the foreground, and the eye glancing
from each to each is raised no more to a far horizon.

The nature of the poet is simple because his inspiration is derived from his delight in or his awe of nature,
from the passion of love, from the heroic deeds of men.

Society becomes complex as its numbers increase, as competition to live grows more severe ; and the minds of men, intent on their relations towards each other, have no leisure for disinterested imaginings. There grows up a science of society, and, according as man is versed in this, is he esteemed among his fellows. Politics, law, commerce, are based not upon eternal principles, but expediency, compromise, evasion. Frederick Harrison has written that when a catastrophe occurs, the practical man of to-day does not " wrestle with his Maker in the spirit," as the Ironsides did. " He flies instantly to human resources, is guided by human science, and staves off suffering and death from thousands by calling in all the resources of learning, foresight, presence of mind, which the Providence of Humanity has trained him to use." In the same way, throughout the nineteenth century the prose writer tended more and more to sup-plant the poet. By the likeness of his form to the daily conversation of men, he approached them as one of themselves : and so meeting them upon familiar ground imperceptibly led them on. The poet wished at once to transport them to the wild lands where he had met with his spiritual adventures. Small wonder if their stiffened minds responded less and less to his call.

" I believe I love poetry almost as much as ever," wrote FitzGerald at the age of forty, " but then I have been suffered to doze all these years in the enjoyment of old childish habits and sympathies, without being called on to more active and serious duties of life. I have not put away childish things, though a man." The basis of poetry is emotion, of prose, logic ; therefore the poet and his audience need experience of the world of the imagination, the prose writer and his audience experience of the world of realities. But the greater the crowds in which men come together, the more com-plex does society become, the harder is experience to attain ; and those who seek it, becoming increasingly preoccupied, dismiss as child's play the fairy regions of the poet. It is said that in Australia there are more readers of poetry than elsewhere, because its gigantic spaces absolve men from the fret of daily contact. Only in solitude can a quality like imaginative vision mature. Subtle harmonies like those of the late books of *Paradise Lost* do not stimulate the mind directly nor with violence. Time must elapse before such words murmured Into the whispering gallery of the soul return in arousing echoes. The inhabitant of the town, by multiplying his daily impressions, has numbed his heart to those rarer and more remote from his material cares, and arrested his spiritual development.

Thus it has come about that in an overcrowded world a man excels his fellows according to his capacity for dealing with accumulated stores of worldly wisdom. And the price he pays for single-minded preoccupation with material things is loss of the sense of the mystery of life. With the decay of religion comes an era of suspicion, when men cease to believe in each other. They dispense with those virtues that are not self-regarding, and they acknowledge the duties of friendship only where there is a common interest.

Above all it is in the commercial classes that the faults of the century culminate. If the object of education is to teach the right values of things, the effect of every profession is to undo this teaching. It would not be difficult to detect the false values of the politician, the lawyer, the schoolmaster. Commerce, which has no other end but to acquire money, has the effect of destroying the moral sense. The honesty of its professors, like the much-vaunted Spartan valour, is a quality imposed from without. They come to believe neither in love nor friendship, nor in anything that has not a financial basis. Theirs is what Ruskin called, vulgarity in its most fatal form, " the inability to feel or conceive noble character or emotion." They decide marriages in their families as they draw up a contract in business. Houston Chamberlain wrote that, " those who do not inherit definite ideals with their blood are neither moral nor immoral, but simply without morals." The failure of the man of commerce to teach right principles to his children is the cause of the growth of an unmoral race.

In FitzGerald's letters we may trace the career of a poet born in a sophisticated world and an age of prose. It may be seen that of all the affections of his youth, conserved so faithfully through early manhood, only his favourite authors remained with him in old age. Rereading Scott's novels at the age of sixty-nine, he confesses that he is " eking them out as charily as I may. For I feel in parting with each, as parting with an old friend whom I may never see again." But unlike other notable letter-writers, as much is to be inferred from his silence as from his confessions. With Cowper and Byron it would be possible to reconstruct their lives from their letters, but not with FitzGerald. He is silent on the deepest subjects, and utters less his hopes and fears. How many readers of Cowper anticipate with joy the visit of his cousin, Lady Hesketh, assured that in her gentle companionship his dread malady will not recur. The darker side of FitzGerald's character is not expressed in his letters ; he does not drain every thought from his soul. The autobiography is of that non-obtrusive kind which is delightful in conversation. When he speaks of himself it is not because he feels the persistent ache of self, but as a mark of confidence in those whom he addresses. Like a man of social virtues, he abstains from subjects of a melancholy cast lest he should damp the spirits of the company. If he introduces a complaint he dismisses it with a jest or comparison : much in the spirit of Robinson Crusoe enumerating the kindnesses of fate on his island. His love for his friends is greater than his love for himself, and his letters are the essence of good conversation.

FitzGerald had a genius for friendship, and at a time of life when the heart is most susceptible to impressions,

he had grouped round him men of the highest intellectual and emotional traits—Spedding, Thackeray, the
Tennysons—to name no others. His life was one of
leisure, free from professional or domestic occupations,
and yet, when Spedding died, he had not seen him for
twenty years ; Thackeray but once in ten years ; and
when Tennyson visited Woodbridge in 1876, it was
twenty years since they had met. In an ordinary man
the reasons would not be far to seek ; but FitzGerald
in old age retained the same love for his friends, and
their images unclouded in his mind's eye.

The first half of his letters are the most delightful
to read, because a larger number are addressed to the
friends of his youth, while in the remainder the more
formal correspondent predominates. At the age of
twenty-six he writes thus to John Allen : " I rejoice
as much as ever in the thought of you, and feel confident
that you will ever be to me the same best of friends
that you ever have been. I owe more to you than all
others put together." And to Frederic Tennyson :
" Don't suppose that this or any other ideal day with
him (Spedding) effaces my days with you." He is the
most objective of letter-writers because he creates an
interest in those to whom and of whom he writes.
Frederic Tennyson becomes of greater account than his
illustrious brother, although the kinsfolk of great men
proverbially lose by comparison. But on no one of the
group is such a glamour shed as Spedding,—to whom,
unhappily, not a single letter has been preserved. Yet
what reader's heart fails to bound when, glancing down
a page, Spedding's name meets his eye ? As the heroes
and heroines in some stories of the Arabian Nights fell
in love with each other by hearsay, so interest grows up
in him by allusion. A certain day that the pair spent
together in London, " has left a taste on my palate
like one of Plato's lighter, easier, and more picturesque
dialogues." And again : " He is one of those I am
well content to make shine at my own expense." When

Spedding chanced to be ill, and a young man of his acquaintance went to sit with him, Fitzgerald wrote : " It really reminds me of some happy Athenian lad privileged to be with Socrates. Some Plato should put down the conversation." Spedding devoted his whole life to an edition of Bacon which should be a vindication. It was but a partial success, and, " I hear that even the wise old Spedding is *mortified* that he has awakened so little interest for his hero. You know his mortification would not be on his own score—— I say this life of his wasted on a vain work is a tragedy pathetic as Antigone or Iphigenia." And some years later on the same theme ; " I declare this is one of the most singular phenomena that has occurred in my day ; a thing to make Montaigne wake from the dead to make an essay upon." Spedding ultimately met with a tragical accident and was carried to St. George's Hospital. " Doctors and nurses all devoted to the patient man." And on his death, FitzGerald thus sums up his character : " He was the wisest man I have ever known : not the less so for plenty of the boy in him ; a great sense of humour, a Socrates in life and death, which he faced with all serenity." In short, " a man that would be incredible had one not known him." That all traces of direct correspondence between the two have disappeared, is indeed a cause for grief. What literary treasure-trove could surpass the discovery of a roll of FitzGerald's letters to him who was called by Carlyle, " the indefatigably patient, placidly invincible and victorious Spedding " ?

Although the determining factor in FitzGerald's seclusion from the world and his friends was his unlucky and short-lived marriage, there are previous signs of the ebb of his self-confidence. As early as 1844 we find him expressing his hatred of London, his conviction that " a great city is a deadly plague." He is surprised that " worth and noble feeling " persist in the country, since railways have mixed us up with metropolitan civilization." More and more the "horror of plunging into London" grows upon him ; and when he does frequent "a party of modern wits," he is glad "to creep into himself and wish himself away, talking to any Suffolk old woman in her cottage." He laments the decline of the "English gentry," "the distinguishing mark and glory of England in history, as the Arts were of Greece, and War of Rome." Some of the happiest hours in FitzGerald's life were spent in his sailing-boat ; and perhaps he loved the sea because it set a term to the ravages of man.

But it was FitzGerald's marriage that finally divided him from the world, and he only partially forgot in later years the shock to his poetical temperament of daily contact with one that was positive and masterful. To find persistent fault with the sensitive is to destroy their belief in themselves and lead them to doubt their right to exist. The letters of FitzGerald's youth are written in high spirits, those of the last twenty-five years of his life have an apologetic tinge. He now only writes to his friends once or twice a year, and now and then he sends out his missive with a fear that it may reach his correspondent at an unseasonable time. "I have really no right to even a yearly response," he writes to Frederic Tennyson ; and a letter to Pollock contains the following message to Spedding : "Pray tell him that I don't now write to him, because I judged that having to answer me hung about his neck like a mill-stone. I am sure all the while that he would answer me by letter and deed if I asked him for any good service." As to a renewal of personal intercourse, the two following passages are specially significant : "I never do invite any of my oldest friends to come and see me, am almost distressed at their proposing to do so. If they take me in their way to, or from, elsewhere . . . it is another matter." "I feel more nervous at the prospect of meeting with an old friend after these years than of any indifferent acquaintance. . . . I feel that I have all to ask and nothing to tell ; and one doesn't like to make a pump of a friend." When Cowell returned from India after an absence of some years, the first essay to re-knit old acquaintance was disappointing. " I hope you don't think I have forgotten you," wrote FitzGerald after their meeting ; " your visit gave me a sad sort of pleasure."

He does not grow bitter because he must relinquish the most poignant joys of his life. It is an inevitable sacrifice to the troubled times in which he lived ; and habits of seclusion, once set going, are not lightly checked. It is not the fault of his friends, and he is wistfully anxious to preserve perfect images of them in his heart. He is glad not to have seen Thackeray of recent years, since he was spoilt by success. He recurs often to this theme, and having heard that Thackeray had " a foible for great folks," he " wonders if this was really so." When Spedding is lying shattered in the hospital he writes : " My dear old Spedding, though I have not seen him these twenty years and more—and probably should never see him again—but he lives—his old self—in my heart of hearts." And to George Borrow : " I like to think over my old friends. There they are, lingering as ineffaceable portraits—done in the prime of life—in my memory. Perhaps we should not like one another so well after a fifteen years separation."

In his youth FitzGerald had been ambitious, but he placed life before art, and valued the love of friends more than the world's applause. Now in later life he realized himself a deedless man, and the equals of former days excelling all round him in their various spheres. It is not strange that a man unlearned in the lore of the world should have shunned personal contact with those who have successfully pushed their fortunes. The one theme of the past on which it would please him to dilate, would have but a remote interest for his hearers ; and he would come to dread that he was hearkened to as a favour.

But no such scruples need oppress him when intercourse was contracted to yearly letters ; and hence,
his later communications abound in exact records of time
and place. "This time twenty years," he writes to
Cowell, "you were going to me at Boulge Cottage :
this time ten years you were preparing for India." To
Carlyle : "I don't like wholly to lose an intercourse
that has lasted more or less these twenty-eight years,
yes, since I was staying with Thackeray and he took
me to Chelsea one night." And now and then comes a
picture in words, as if the author roused himself to bridge
the gulf between hearts by pointing to at least one vivid
experience in common saved from the wreck of years.
Writing to Mrs. Charles Allen : "And all the *place*
at Freestone. I can walk about it as I lie awake here,
and see the very yellow flowers in the fields, and hear
that distant sound of explosion in some distant quarry."
And to Tennyson's wife, after the death of Spedding :
"And dear J. S. at Mirehouse where your husband and
I stayed, very near upon fifty years ago, in 1835 it was,
in the month of May, when the daffodil was out in a
field before the house, as I see them, though not in such
force, owing to the cold winds, before my window now.
Does A. T. remember them ?"

A critic once wittily remarked that FitzGerald brought
to Posh what he brought to Omar. It was the simplicity
of his character which impelled him towards the boatman,
as it had hindered him from keeping pace with his swifter-
moving friends. "If he *should* turn out knave, I shall
have done with all faith in my own judgment," he wrote ;
and many of his letters are filled with extravagant eulogies
of Posh. "You can't think what a grand, tender soul
this is, lodged in a suitable carcase. . . ." "I want a
good big head of the fellow, to hang up by old Thackeray
and Tennyson, all three having a stamp of grandeur
about them in their several ways, and occupying great
places in my soul." "His simplicity of soul . . . justice
of thought, tenderness of nature, and all the other good

gifts which make him a gentleman of nature's grandest
type." " I thought that both Tennyson and Thackeray
were inferior to him in respect of thinking of themselves."
Whatever verdict may be passed on Posh's simplicity
of soul, there is no doubt of FitzGerald's. He confided
to Posh his innermost secrets, and even discussed his
unhappy marriage.

Had FitzGerald been born a hundred years earlier
he might have realized his immortality on earth. The
London of the eighteenth century would not have
repelled him as did the London of the nineteenth. As
a member of the Literary Club that revolved round
Dr. Johnson, he would have retained the same friends
and interests in old age. For FitzGerald was not akin
to Wordsworth in his love of wild country, and elected
to live " in a small house just outside a pleasant English
town." In later years we find him writing : " I am
afraid to leave the poor town with its little bustle ! As
one grows older, lonelier and sadder, is not the little town
best ? " What he feared was the portentous growth of
the town which had followed the industrial revolution :
the miles of dreary streets that meet the eye of the railway
traveller as he draws near London ; the rows of factory
chimneys polluting with their smoke once beautiful
scenes ; and the swarming millions called out of the
unknown to serve these terrible engines. Above all,
he feared the suspicion sown in the human heart, the
ideas and manners of the commercial classes, the decline
of reverence for birth and culture, and the evils of democratic institutions. And, not least, the altered scale of
values engendered by the increased pressure on the
means of subsistence : faith in the unseen—the former
stay of character—displaced by knowledge of the
psychology of associated men.

To resist such tendencies would seem to FitzGerald
as futile as the effort to stem the advance of the Atlantic.
He was not to be won by the specious pleadings for
return to nature of Rousseau and his fellow-senti-

mentalists. Browning once counselled a friend to abuse railways but to use them ; and FitzGerald well knew that the fever in the blood which had sprung from modern conditions was not to be exorcised by a theory. But minds like his are not dejected by the thought that an end will come of man's doings on earth. To him and some others, stories of the mounds of Babylon and of mighty cities which have arisen and flourished, and of which no traces remain, do not come amiss. There is even something consoling in the thought of Macaulay's New Zealander who is to take his stand on a broken arch of London Bridge to sketch the ruins of St. Paul's.

Goldsmith once wrote that the fear of death may easily be borne, because its coming is uncertain. This is less true of the fear of life, because life is about and around us ; and he who knows this fear need only walk into an unfamiliar street or open a newspaper to be struck to the heart by some untoward sign. We are told that the best antidote is " to cultivate one's garden," to occupy one's self with " the mastery of some definite task," that " it is when men neglect their work and whisper together in clubs and public places that they become panic-stricken."[1] But this doctrine presses hardly on those to whom fortune allots no straw to make their bricks : the poet or artist, whose faculty does not depend on will.

That FitzGerald suffered from the fear of life is to be inferred from his retreat from the world and his scanty poetical output. He must have shuddered at the growing town, as the cultured Roman of the Empire shuddered at the thought of the barbarian hordes lurking in the German forests. He turned from a world whence beauty had departed, and where the human spirit had been tethered to the material plane ; but, unlike Scott, he could not forget the hideous present in the romantic past. He conserved the memory of what he had seen, and the result was to freeze his creative springs. His

[1] *The Times,* October 3rd, 1910.

was no rage or hatred of man, like Swift's, but something akin to the anxious fears of Pascal for the human race, joined to fear for himself, that he was looked upon as a drone in the gigantic hive of modern industry. Unconscious of having produced an immortal work in the *Omar*, he almost apologises for his life of leisure. And yet he was so simple-natured, so easily pleased, and by such a hair's-breadth did he miss happiness, that his speculations of delight in ideal regions are always accompanied by a backward look at the world which he is leaving. It is this spirit which informs the most wistful stanza of the *Omar* :—

> " Ah Love ! could you and I with Him conspire
> To grasp this sorry Scheme of Things entire,
> Would not we shatter it to bits—and then
> Remould it nearer to the Heart's Desire ! "

Boswell

BOSWELL

WAS it Steele who wrote, in the character of a disappointed man, that all his life he had struggled for the applause of the world and won nothing but its ridicule ? How nearly such a fate has befallen Boswell must be plain to all students of the history of the Johnsonian epic. Gray's mischievous saying that " any fool may write a most valuable book by chance, if he will only tell us what he heard and said with veracity," and Macaulay's ill-natured essay, have established in the heart of the general reader a prejudice against Boswell. Despite Carlyle, despite critics such as Leslie Stephen and Mr. Percy Fitzgerald, there is still something of novelty in the assertion that Boswell was a genius.

The art of the biographer is to set forth the inner character of his subject, and therefore Boswell and Plutarch are pre-eminent. But that wherein Boswell stands alone is that he has made biography the means of realization of self. The widespread prejudice against him has hindered the recognition of the true significance of this. Many who would acclaim De Quincey or Sir Thomas Browne for the intimacy of their personal revelations have denounced Boswell for shamelessness and vanity.

Boswell's methods of composition are themselves a refutation of those who believe with Gray. His connection with Johnson lasted for more than twenty years, during which time he never ceased to amass material for the life, and to note down conversations which had

taken place at the Mitre or Literary Club, or any other
favourite resort. It was not till after the sage's death
that he began to recast his abundant material ; and
when he took pen in hand, the great figure of Johnson
had moved nearer to his spiritual vision. Jowett observed
that nothing in Aristophanes is more truly Aristophanic
than the speech which Plato puts into his mouth in the
Symposium, as to the origin of the sexes ; and such
is the impression left by Boswell's conjecture of what
Johnson's reply would have been to a formal invitation
to the Wilkes dinner : " Dine with Jack Wilkes, sir ;
I'd as soon dine with Jack Ketch ! " Boswell's book is
no mere transcript of reality, but the work of his subconscious mind ; no monument of skilful reporting,
but a record of imaginative insight into a great character.
He had outwardly preserved Johnson's speeches and
acts in his note book, and then dismissed them into the
depths of his being. When after years they emerged
into the light of day, and were subjected to the revision
of the conscious mind, they had suffered the sea change.
It was a vindication of Carlyle's saying, " Out of silence
comes thy strength."

And yet, the *Life of Johnson*, in spite of its success,
was for many years denied the attribute of greatness.
Boswell's ghost might be pleased to learn that the
causes which retarded his reputation were akin to those
which retarded Shakespeare's. The same criticism which
condemned *Macbeth* as a mixture of horrors and
platitudes assessed the immortal biography merely as a
work of entertainment. Shakespeare's character is a
mystery because he allows no personal whim to come
between himself and his characters ; and Boswell's
vanity never hinders his rendering of essential truth.
It is the universality in both writers which makes the
whole of Shakespeare and portions of Boswell more like
a natural force than the work of individual genius.

The prejudice against Boswell—which his ill-regulated
life had much to do in promoting—has hindered a true

appreciation of his character as well as his work. It is needless to repeat the countless harsh epithets which have been applied to one of the most lovable of English authors. Much is forgiven to the man of genius, and every characteristic trait of genius was Boswell's ; but as the perfection of his art blinded the public to its merits, so it was with his character, and therefore he is not forgiven. Macaulay and many others have formed wrong estimates through arguing backwards from some more than usually heinous act committed in public. Only shall we reach the truth when we start from the assumption that Boswell had the emotional instability of the man of genius.

We speak of the " simplicity " of great men until the phrase, like many another, loses its meaning by repetition. The truth is that if a great man is simple it is in every other department of life but that which concerns his greatness. Power does not arise suddenly, but is evolved from small beginnings ; and evolution—if Herbert Spencer's definition be still admitted—is progress from the simple to the complex, from the homogeneous to the heterogeneous. Napoleon and Bismarck were simple in their domestic relations, and it is believed that both were excellent husbands and fathers ; but their tactical and political faculties did not spring from the emotional nature. The gifts which make a poet are those of the heart rather than the head ; his complexity is of the emotional nature ; and he is as often an indifferent man of the world as an indifferent family man. The Philistine is far more likely to love once and once only, than the poet who, with Sterne, must never be without a Dulcinea.

It is convenient to apply the word " poet " to all imaginative writers, independent of the accident of form ; and we will speak of Boswell as having the poetic temperament. It is admitted that the possessor of this temperament is out of touch with the real world, and the cause is not alone that he is rapt in a world of ideals.

For knowledge reaches the brain through the gateway of the feelings, and practical knowledge can be better discriminated by the simple than the complex emotional nature. The failure of the poet in business or politics is explained by one of the oldest truths in the world : the subjectivity of all knowledge.

Where there is sensibility there is imagination, and as the impression comes, the flash of imagination lights up no single highway of action, but a multitude of lanes ; and the bewildered poet flies to others, and begs them to choose for him. He becomes abnormally sensitive to suggestion, and of this the extremest instance is Romney, who abandoned his wife because Sir Joshua Reynolds said that an artist had better be unmarried. Similarly, when Johnson expressed a strong wish to see the Great Wall of China, Boswell, who had never before thought on the subject, at once caught the enthusiasm. And he once requested Johnson to furnish him with a list of arguments in favour of Christianity, that he might never feel uneasy when his faith was attacked. Among such numberless channels is the incoming tide distributed that the poet cannot prefer one or two, as does the ordinary man.

A contrast will illustrate the Boswellian strength and weakness. He once complained that after a supper with Johnson his head had ached from the effect of wine. " It was not the wine," said Johnson, " that made your head ache, but the sense that I put into it " ; on which Boswell asked, in genuine surprise, " Will sense make the head ache ? " From the naivete of this question let us turn to the insight of the following passage from one of his *Hypocondriac* essays : " I am not at all clear that evils, when they actually happen, will be less felt by us from having contemplated them long before. They will come loaded with additional darkness from the clouds of imagination, and if the mind be weakened and worn by fanciful sufferings, it will be less able to bear a severe shock than if it met it with that sound vigour which is produced by security and happiness."

Even when, like Bacon, the poet is steeped to the lips in theoretical worldly wisdom, it seems to avail him little ; as witness Bacon's downfall from the chancellorship, the disorder of his private life, and his inability to restrain his servants. The affairs of the world demand instantaneous decisions, and, at times, disregard of the opinions and the susceptibilities of others ; and here the poet finds he has assumed a character which he cannot sustain. He is overmuch incensed by rudeness, or grateful for consideration. One of the maxims for success in life is " Never apologise " ; but if he commits rough actions it is in a hesitating manner, which unfixes him in the estimation of his fellows as a serious rival, and in the respect of inferiors. Or should he win a victory, so great will be his compunction for his fallen foe that he will abandon the spoils. His capacity for feeling is not necessarily more intensive than those about him, but certainly more extensive ; and hence he can be turned even from a righteous cause by an air of conviction in an opponent or an assumption of distress. The self-assurance of the average man lies in his incapacity for extensive feeling.

The world marvels at Shakespeare's imagining of the fool side by side with Lear, but censures Boswell for introducing quotations from the devotional Ogden in the midst of a drinking-bout. It admires Donne's comparison of himself and his beloved to a pair of compasses, but sneers at Boswell when, having written an account of his wife's death to his friend Temple in a truly heartbroken strain, he concludes : " There were nineteen carriages followed the hearse, and a large body of horsemen and the tenants of all my lands." The distinguishing faculty of the poet is to feel many things simultaneously, and its literary expression is metaphor.

Lombroso denied to the man of genius both tact and moderation. The second of these strictures is too obvious to need comment ; the first may be partially accepted, if " tact " implies that quality by which a man attains his own end without giving offence. It is the difficulties in their own natures that have made the wisest poets of the modern world pass their lives in retirement, and shun the disasters that have attended those of their company who have attempted to take part in the business of life. And because of this disability we are told that the poet remains an eternal child. The comparison illustrates not only the poetic simplicity, but also its complexity ; for among worldlings the boy is emotionally more developed than the man. As years pass on, the current is confined more and more to one or two well-worn channels. " 'Tis an error, surely, to talk of the simplicity of youth," says Thackeray. " I think no persons are more hypocritical, and have a more affected behaviour to one another, than the young. They deceive themselves and each other with artifices that do not impose upon men of the world ; and so we get to understand truth better, and grow simpler as we grow older."

Hypocrisy and self-deception are unjust charges against men of poetic genius ; for hypocrisy is the assumption of a feeling, and not, as in the case of the poet, its imaginative recall. " I have endeavoured to feel what I ought to feel," wrote Coleridge on one occasion ; and the phrase throws a flood of light on the peculiar temperament. We hear that Sheridan, on becoming acquainted with Warren Hastinsg, exclaimed expansively that the speech he had delivered against him at the impeachment was dictated by political necessity. " Will you make that public ? " replied the practical man of affairs ; and Sheridan was at once abashed. It will be remembered that, after eloping with Mary Wollstonecraft, Shelley wrote to the forsaken Harriet urging her to join them in Switzerland, " where you will at last find one firm and constant friend to whom your interests will be always dear—by whom your feelings will never wilfully be injured." Matthew Arnold explained the causes of this proceeding to be " an entirely human inflammability, joined to an inhuman want of humour and a superhuman power of self-deception." Yet, if we keep in mind the intricacy of the poet's emotional organization, something of our virtuous anger will be remitted even in the case of Shelley. It is tempting to think that even the great Chatham may be numbered among the unknowing in the affairs of men, and that he affected social retirement through inability to hold his own. He was unversed, it is said, in financial or commercial matters, and even in the procedure of the House of Commons. Lecky tells how there was little close argument in his speeches, that " he delighted in touching the moral chords, in appealing to strong passions, and in arguing questions on high grounds of principle rather than on grounds of detail."

Knowledge of business is said to consist in mastery of detail, but of all knowledge the same may be said. There are emotional facts equally with business facts ; and to the poet the man of business is as much a child in the emotional world. Complexity implies departure from rule, and where a child could have grasped the rule, the exceptions demand a much-developed nature. But the poet, when he is playing for a worldly stake, will learn his rules by heart, and adhere to them with a pertinacity which will draw down upon him the ridicule of all who can discriminate. No doubt Boswell had heard of men rising in the world through patronage, and he was familiar with the saying that perseverance overcomes all obstacles. All through his life, therefore, he sought the acquaintance of those who might serve him, without clear conception of what the service was to be. We are told that Bacon was " the most importunate and untiring of suitors," but he differed from Boswell in having a more definite aim.

Some poets—notably the Lake School—have been content to live their lives apart ; but renunciation is not effected without a struggle, and to the imaginative

mind the world has much that is alluring. The poet
may court disaster in politics, like Dante or Milton ;
he may speak unguardedly, like Byron or Pater, and so
damage his reputation. For eccentricity is born of the
wish to shine, and of despair of emulating those with
" strong personalities," who push their fortunes with
success, and whose strength is built upon emotional
narrowness. The most painful disharmony is the wish
of the poet to excel in a world for which he is unfit. As
this globe consists more of water than land—an argument
used against design in creation—so the nature of the poet
is given over to change and tempest, and remains in-
hospitable to the human settler.

In the Athens of Pericles, or the England of Elizabeth,
the poet might still consort with the great upon equal
terms ; but Boswell lived in the reign of George III,
when the foundations of the modern world were laid.
The characteristic of a utilitarian age is co-operation,
the undertaking of gigantic enterprises by the union
of many hands and minds. The man of feeling, who
thinks to capture this highly organized modern world,
mistakes it for a Jericho round which he is to walk blow-
ing his trumpet till its walls fall flat. There is a tendency
to externalize all values ; even rank, without wealth, is
looked upon with less and less respect. We are told
to mistrust every impulse lest we should jar this complex
machine of modern life. No less must charity be
bestowed through recognized agencies, with the result
of what the more thoughtful journalists call " spiritual
leanness." Into so many departments has the business
of life become specialized that mastery of the whole is
impracticable. When men meet together their conversation is limited to material facts ; and he is valued who
can show the point under discussion in its relation to
the vast social structure. But the poet is overcome by
the predominance of the external world, and like a very
child sits mute. He will either decline the combat by
agreeing with each in turn or lose his temper.

Carlyle, whose ideas were primitive, has said that no great man has ever been troubled by the wish to shine ; but Boswell was born into an age when greatness must be ratified by the popular vote. A life of security in towns has caused religious fears to yield to the tyranny of custom, and each seeks the approval of his fellow-men rather than his conscience. But the poet, whose social sense is abnormally developed, treats the whole world as he would his family, and reveals himself in all his weaknesses with implicit trust in its tolerance. When Boswell was in Berlin and wished to visit Italy, he requested the British Ambassador to unite in supplicating his father for the required funds. Dignity is hardly preserved by him who can scarcely open his lips without self-revelation, and who gives another the advantage of acquaintance with his inner thoughts. The sympathies of the poet extend to all, irrespective of age or station in life or character ; and by the love or hate of the lowest of mortals can he be cheered or wounded. Boswell was no poet as Spenser or Shelley were poets. The life of London as it was sufficed him ; and had there been a throne for him among those of statesmen or generals or great authors, he could have dispensed with an ideal scheme.

The errors which have undone Boswell are those of the typical man of genius ; the emotional instability, the predominance of the world of ideas over the world of realities, the deficiency in tact, the over-developed social sense. How characteristic is the letter to Erskine, written in his twenty-second year, wherein he sets forth the hopes and ambitions of his life ! He is to enjoy brilliant scenes of happiness as an officer of the guards ; lured to this regiment, no doubt, by the splendour of its uniform. Ministers of State and ladies of quality are to seek his acquaintance ; dukes to invite him to their country seats ; and there he is to acquire a perfect knowledge of men and manners, and form friendships with the learned and ingenious in every science. He is to make a triumphal tour through Europe, and gather honours at every court. He is to become a greater orator than Pitt, repel a Spanish invasion at the head of his regiment, and marry a lady with a hundred thousand pounds. His children are to be worthy of their glorious father ; and when he dies, statues are to be erected to his immortal honour. . Yet this rhapsody has a strange conclusion. " I am thinking that my mind is too delicate and my feelings too fine for the rough bustle of life. I——shall steal silently and unperceived through the world——"

The poetic nature is proverbially one of extremes, and Boswell's love of the life of towns amounted to a passion. It has been justly said that when he visited the Hebrides with Johnson, their object was not the enjoyment of scenery, but the spectacle of men and manners. The only excellence which he was fitted to attain was literary, but he was dazzled by the pageant of the world and dissipated his energies in quest of social or political distinction His dependence on the verdict of others is amusingly illustrated by a footnote in the *Tour to the Hebrides* : " My great grandfather . . . was Alexander, Earl of Kincardine . . . From him the blood of Bruce flows in my veins. Of such ancestry who would not be proud ? And, as *Nihil est, nisi hoc sciat alter*, is peculiarly true of genealogy, who would not be glad to seize a fair opportunity to let it be known ? " Again, in his second *Letter to the People of Scotland*, he turns the stream of politics into personal channels, such as his affection for his wife, the degree of his courage, his *noctes atticæ* with Goldsmith and Reynolds. It recalls Mark Pattison's stricture on Milton's method in the Morus controversy ; how, instead of stating the case of the republic, " he holds Europe listening to an account of himself, his accomplishments, his studies and travels, his stature, the colour of his eyes, his skill in fencing, etc."

It is unfortunate that we know nothing of Boswell's mother beyond the single record that she was " a woman of almost unexampled piety and goodness." Lord Auchinleck, though not harsh in deeds, was at least harsh in words ; and it was doubtless maternal indulgence that prevented Boswell's spirit from being crushed in childhood, and so retrieved the gaiety of succeeding generations. The temperaments of Boswell and his father were antipodean, the latter being narrow, unemotional, and practical ; and his last years were embittered by his son's failure in serious business. With his influence and connections, Boswell might have attained to some eminence at the Scottish Bar, but all his sympathies drew him to London, and he essayed in vain to make an opening for himself at the English Bar. We cannot but commiserate the old Laird when we reflect how far he was from divining the true cause of this sacrifice of opportunity to whim, viz., the supremacy of the internal world.

To a nature like Boswell's, encouragement was essential, and had he encountered a series of rebuffs in youth, he might never have Johnsonized the land. It was his adventure in Corsica and his success in winning the friendship of Paoli that gave him a position in London society. In his vague wish for distinction he had turned his steps to Corsica because it was unknown to his fellow-countrymen. From that time, as all his critics have remarked, his diffidence in the presence of the great vanished. On his return to London he gazed undaunted into the eagle face of Chatham ; and the words in which he suggested a familiar correspondence with that minister are too well known for quotation. Yet in the preface to his book on Corsica there occurs a self-revealing passage, where he admits himself out of touch with real life. He acknowledges his desire for the fame of an author as the means of " establishing himself as a respectable character in distant society, without any danger of having that character lessened by the observation of his weaknesses. To preserve a uniform dignity among those who see us every day is hardly possible. . . . The author of an approved book may allow his natural disposition an easy play, and yet indulge the pride of superior genius . . ."

To live his romance rather than to write it was Boswell's aim, and his faculty of " make believe " was worthy of the eternal child. He delighted in assuming the dress of a Corsican chief, and when he visited Chatham to entreat help for Corsica, it was in that garb. He sang to an audience of Corsican sailors a translation of " Hearts of Oak," and as they joined in the chorus he imagined himself a recruiting sea-officer. At Fort George the drum beat for dinner, and it pleased him for the moment to be a military man. We must seek a parallel in Lamb who, strolling about Oxford in the Long Vacation, became Master of Arts, or Seraphic Doctor, as the spirit moved him ; or rose at the chapel-bell, and dreamt that it rang for him. The effect of music on Boswell was to produce alternate sensations of pathetic dejection, and daring resolution which inclined him to rush into the thickest part of the battle. And his regard for Johnson was such that on one occasion, " I thought I could defend him at the point of my sword." Nor must be omitted the famous scene at Inverary Castle, when the " gay inviting appearance " of the ladies' maids, " tripping about in neat morning dresses," made such an impression on his fancy that he " could have been a knight-errant for them."

It is small wonder that cooling breezes blew from the land of material facts upon Boswell's imaginative ardour. He failed in his profession, he mismanaged his financial affairs, and contrived to run into debt. He was pathetically anxious for his father to increase his allowance ; but Lord Auchinleck, who was bound for the £1000, which his son owed, reduced it by £100 ; on which Boswell exclaims that his father " is really a strange man." Many of the letters to his friend Temple contain allusions to the terms on which he stands with his father. He writes : " How happy should I be to get an independency by my own influence while my father is alive." And again : " He has a method of treating me which makes me feel myself like a timid boy," which to Boswell "(comprehending all that my character does in my own imagination) is intolerable." Or, " How galling is it to the friend of Paoli to be treated so ! "

Boswell's career illustrates the failure of the man of poetic genius to hold his own against less gifted denizens of the material world. His intercourse with Temple's younger brother is truly characteristic of him and his tribe. " I have unluckily allowed him to be too free with me ; and I own it hurts me when I find my folly bringing me into the situation of being upon an equality with, if not below, the young man." Pope could be incited to fury by the meanest Grub Street scribbler ; and it has been said of Hans Andersen that he was too much of a child himself to be wholly fond of children. We find Boswell censuring as injudicious the custom of introducing children after dinner, and allowing them " to poison the moments of festivity by attracting the attention of the company." That nation is most vulnerable which has the widest territory ; and the emotional system of the poet, like a long and scantily guarded seaboard, offers landing to the feeblest invader.

In the life of towns the fittest to survive are the unemotional. Not the least of Boswell's mortifications was that he could not get the world to take him seriously. He wished in vain to attach himself to the Ministry and to enter Parliament ; and when Johnson died, the booksellers entrusted the official biography to other hands, although Boswell's *Tour to the Hebrides* had been published with success. In connecting himself with Johnson, Boswell found a means of indirectly satisfying his craving for consideration ; and it is to the lovable qualities in Johnson's nature that we owe the duration of the tie. Had the stage of Paoli's exploits been England, had Chatham " found time to honour him with a letter," had Pitt's ear been less obdurate to the

strains of the " Grocer of London," Boswell's worship
might have been diffused among various idols.

Johnson was a " friendly " man, and the virtue which
he most honoured was sincerity. It was his own possession of it that made Carlyle enrol him among the
Heroes ; and because Boswell was fundamentally
sincere, he was accepted of Johnson. Much exaggeration has attended the rebukes which Johnson administered
to his follower ; and, if they have survived, it is because
of their intrinsic wit. The truth is that of the two
Johnson had most to forgive, in the assiduities of one
who had neither moderation nor worldly tact. We know
the kind of questions with which he plied the sage,
such as " Why is an apple round and a pear pointed ? "
and if, in addition to their absurdity, we presume that
Boswell was indiscreet in the choice of his questioning-
time, it is natural that Johnson now and then determined
to snub him in public. " The man compels me to treat
him so," he said, after one outburst ; and having glanced
through the pages of Boswell's *Tour to the Hebrides*, he
observed : " One would think the man had been hired
to be a spy upon me."

Johnson was Boswell's greatest asset in his ambitious
schemes. It was not his acquaintance that sufficed
Boswell, but a friendship of that esoteric kind which
might exist between kinsfolk ; for it is only when free
scope is given to the emotional nature that the man of
poetic genius can hold his own. Therefore, in the early
stages, he was jealous of Goldsmith's privilege to be
invited to Johnson's house to drink tea with Mrs.
Williams ; and when the favour was extended to
himself he grasped it eagerly. Since he could not shine
by his own prowess he would do so indirectly through
that of his friend, and receive the same kind of homage
that is accorded to the family of a great man. The
superstition that Boswell was taxed to the utmost limit
of his endurance in his discipleship of Johnson still
needs some dispelling. To refute it one must remember

Johnson's dependence on his fellow-creatures, his hypochondria, and dread of solitude. The letter in which he conveyed the news of his wife's death affected the recipient as the strongest expression of grief he had ever heard. It was his habit to accompany his visitors down the stairs as far as the street door, in the hope that they might turn back. The partial success of his visit to Boswell's house is well known, and no one deplored it more than Johnson. " I know that Mrs. Boswell does not love me," was the burden of his letters to Boswell thenceforth ; and here are some extracts which prove that years afterwards the incident was still fresh in his mind : " I am glad that my old enemy, Mrs. Boswell, begins to feel some remorse." " I was pleased to be told that I accused Mrs. Boswell unjustly, in supposing that she bears me ill-will." " Make my compliments to Mrs. Boswell, who is, I hope, reconciled to me, and to the young people whom I have never offended." To Mrs. Boswell he had previously written : " Do not teach the young ones to dislike me, as you dislike me yourself." No one was more scrupulous to keep friendships in repair than Johnson ; he counted a year wasted in which he made no new friend ; and so far from just tolerating Boswell, he grappled him to his heart with hoops of steel. " If I were to lose Boswell, it would be a limb amputated," is his reported saying ; and the fact that the following sentences, scattered among a correspondence of years, have been preserved by the man whose praises they celebrate, does not lessen their value : " I consider your friendship as a possession which I intend to hold till you take it from me, and to lament if ever by my fault I should lose it." " Do not neglect to write to me, for your kindness is one of the pleasures of my life, which I should be sorry to lose." " I have heard you mentioned as a man whom everybody likes." " I love every part about you—but your affectation of distress." " Were I in distress, there is no man to whom I should sooner come than to you." And these two sayings, which Johnson delivered to Boswell at the time of his last illness, are well worth pondering : " You must be as much with me as you can. You have done me good. You cannot think how much better I am since you came in." " Boswell, I think I am easier with you than with almost anybody." In the exchange of provocations, nothing can exceed Boswell's behaviour to Johnson at Miss Monckton's reception, when, entering the room in a state of intoxication, he placed himself next to Johnson and addressed him in a boisterous manner, to let the company know how he could contend with Ajax. When he made a penitential call upon the sage a few days later, he was received with the most " friendly gentleness." Yet the world still believes with Carlyle that insult was Boswell's daily portion.

It is hard to credit, according to latest theories, that Boswell wrote the *Life of Johnson* solely with the purpose of self-aggrandisement. His repeated requests for expressions of Johnson's good will, his meticulous fears on one occasion that he was too easy in his presence, and missed " that awful reverence with which he used to contemplate Mr. Samuel Johnson," reveal genuine love. Perhaps the truth is that there was, within the width of Boswell's emotional nature, affection side by side with the desire to shelter himself behind the buttress of Johnson's fame. The failure of the poet to carry weight in the counsels of men leads him to adopt the device of using his great friends as weapons. Aware that he is not taken seriously, he will rather quote the opinion of others than express his own disapproval. Thus we find Boswell repeating to Hume the saying of Temple that he was the Government's " infidel pensioner " ; to Foote that of Johnson that he was an infidel as a dog is an infidel because he had never thought on the subject of religion ; to Lord Monboddo Johnson's sarcasm that he talked nonsense without knowing it ; and many others. Both the *Tour of the Hebrides* and the *Life of Johnson* called forth a storm of protest because of their treatment of living persons. The hospitality which Boswell received on his journey he repaid with fault-finding and even abuse. Having on one occasion mischievously persuaded his hostess to offer Dr. Johnson a cold sheep's head for breakfast, he remarked that " Sir Allan seemed displeased at his sister's vulgarity." At Sir John Dalrymple's, they " went to bed in ancient rooms, which would have better suited the climate of Italy in summer, than that of Scotland in the month of November." From the *Life* one might select many more of these indiscretions ; and even the excellent Langton is treated with some patronage. The truth is that when Boswell took pen in hand he felt himself in a position to repay the slights he had received as he went to and fro in the world. The voice of the poet may be drowned in the tumult of lesser men ; but in the seclusion of the study he can shape with effect those sentences which a nervous manner has disarmed. He can apportion praise and blame at his will, and those who would have scoffed at his oral judgments are now struck in the joints of their armour.

It will be remembered that Boswell repeated to Johnson his wife's saying that she had often seen a bear led by a man, but never a man led by a bear ; and that Johnson in consequence hastened his departure from their house. Obviously, this belongs to a different category from the indiscretions already noted, since to neither of these persons did Boswell wish to give offence. He repeated it as an instance of his wife's humour, and he expected Johnson to enjoy the joke. Similarly, scattered through the *Life*, are numberless aspersions on living men set down without intent to harm ; and the storm which they raised surprised no one more than Boswell. The explanation is that Boswell conceived imaginatively of Johnson and his circle—as Homer did the siege of Troy, or Shakespeare the history of England. His work is that of the poet, not the reporter ; and in his anxiety to body forth the vision that was within him, he neglected the laws of the external world.

That Boswell inadvertently treated himself with equal roughness is obvious to all. Mention has been made of the effect of music on himself, in his own words. To this Johnson replied, " If it made me such a fool I should never hear it." Boswell was totally unconscious that the speech applied to himself, and he pursued the subject in yet further detail. Again, one of the most notorious episodes of the Hebrides journey was Boswell's riot at Corrichatachin. Next day he nervously anticipated Johnson's visit to his bedside, but when that event occurred, he was much relieved by the sage's " indulgence " and " jocularity,"—whereas, to the ordinary reader, he appears ironically contemptuous. So autocratic a father is the poet's wish to his thought, so deluding are the gleams which imagination throws across the hard road of life.

Mr. Percy Fitzgerald has shown conclusively that Boswell and Johnson were not on terms of friendship at the time of the latter's death ; and he regrets the lost picture of the final scene that Boswell would have drawn. Boswell was unlike Johnson, who was ready to forgive angry expressions ; and it is probable that words spoken in haste and suffered to grow cold were re-animated by his imagination, as the frozen viper in the countryman's bosom. There had been previous periods of separation when Boswell had brooded over offences, till the memory of former scenes of festivity again filled his mind, and he hastened up to London. The imaginative are prone to resentment, for theirs is the power of calling up scenes and reapplying words ; and these, removed from the amenities of human intercourse, work like poison in the system.

The sorrows of the man of genius were experienced by Boswell in full measure. A prey to ambition from earliest youth, he saw men of meaner capacity passing him in the race. In his forty-ninth year he wrote to Temple that he was " constitutionally unfit for any employment." When his wife died, he was faced with the problem of directing the lives of his children. " While she lived, I had no occasion almost to think concerning my family . . . I am the most helpless of human beings." It is not surprising that his eldest son began to " oppose " him. His affairs were involved, his constitution was yielding to habits of intemperance, there was no practice at the Bar, and no seat in Parliament. It was indeed : " O Temple ! Temple ! is this realising any of the towering hopes which have so often been the subject of our conversations and letters ? " He did live to see the success of his great biography, but there is an uncertainty about the fate of all original works,—and how long it has been in finding true estimation !

The characters of the world are frequently compared with those of fiction. There is one trait in Bottom the Weaver which recalls the side of Boswell expressed in the memorable letter to Erskine. " Let me play Thisby, too," " Let me play the lion, too," exclaims Bottom, as he foresees their opportunities to win applause. But there is something in the closing scene of Boswell's life which recalls not the least beautiful deathbed in fiction. In *Esmond*, Lord Castlewood dies " with a blessing on his lips, and love and repentance and kindness in his manly heart." And so, the last letter which Boswell wrote, or rather dictated, through weakness, to his life-long friend, concluded thus : " God bless you, my dear Temple ! I ever am your old and affectionate friend here, and, I trust, hereafter."